Building Intelligent Cloud Applications

*Develop Scalable Models Using
Serverless Architectures with Azure*

Vicente Herrera García and John Biggs

Beijing · Boston · Farnham · Sebastopol · Tokyo

Building Intelligent Cloud Applications

by Vicente Herrera García and John Biggs

Copyright © 2019 O'Reilly Media, Inc. All rights reserved.

Published by O'Reilly Media, Inc., 1005 Gravenstein Highway North, Sebastopol, CA 95472.

O'Reilly books may be purchased for educational, business, or sales promotional use. Online editions are also available for most titles (*http://oreilly.com*). For more information, contact our corporate/institutional sales department: 800-998-9938 or *corporate@oreilly.com*.

Editors: Rachel Roumeliotis and Nicole Tache

Production Editor: Kristen Brown

Copyeditor: Octal Publishing Services, LLC

Proofreader: Rachel Head

Indexer: Judith McConville

Interior Designer: David Futato

Cover Designer: Karen Montgomery

Illustrator: Rebecca Demarest

April 2019:   First Edition

Revision History for the First Edition

2019-04-25:   First Release
2019-09-10:   Second Release

See *http://oreilly.com/catalog/errata.csp?isbn=9781492052326* for release details.

The O'Reilly logo is a registered trademark of O'Reilly Media, Inc. *Building Intelligent Cloud Applications*, the cover image of an azure jay, and related trade dress are trademarks of O'Reilly Media, Inc.

978-1-492-05232-6

[LSI]

Table of Contents

Part I.   Cloud-Based Development

Preface

The past few years have brought massive changes to the way we think about applications. As products scaled to a global level, developers worked hard to keep up, creating new paradigms that left behind the complex client–server systems that were then in place. The resulting systems are called *serverless applications*, and they will be the primary focus of this book.

Most applications require computing resources, databases, and hardware. The assumption behind a program in Django, for example, is that it will be deployed in an environment that is similar or superior to the environment in which it was coded. It's also assumed that the program will be on all the time, using resources and running up a bill.

A serverless program is, in essence, a system that requires no infrastructure management, allowing the programmer to focus primarily on the business logic or functionality of the program. It is a bold change in the world of program design, and it's becoming more and more popular.

To understand the implications of this model, you need to have an understanding of the basic ideas that underlie functional programming. We'll review them in Chapter 2.

Intelligent Serverless Applications

There are many different meanings, often overlapping, attributed to the terms "artificial intelligence" and "machine learning." In this book, we concern ourselves with the ways in which we can use algorithms to find patterns hidden in large datasets—patterns that would be difficult or impossible for humans to detect without the help of computers. There are various ways in which we can set algorithms to adjust themselves to improve their performance upon each iteration. This is called *machine learning*.

Serverless applications and functional programming lend themselves perfectly to the exploration of these systems, and in this book you will learn how to build machine learning applications using a serverless architecture.

How This Book Is Organized

First, we should note that this book focuses on Azure, Microsoft's cloud platform. The concepts we discuss here are universal, but our examples describe how to implement them in Azure.

The book comprises eight chapters divided into three parts.

Part I, *Cloud-Based Development*, lays out the idea of "serverless applications" and explains how *event-driven apps* are built up from self-contained function calls hosted in the cloud. This part explains the APIs that are the interface between your locally running program and the cloud-based machine learning and data-manipulation services.

Part II, *Adding Intelligence*, discusses the role of data and how you make it available to your programs. The very essence of "intelligence" in cloud-based applications comes from the use of various machine learning techniques and models to interrogate large datasets. You don't need to build your own models; you just need to understand which ones best address the problem you're trying to solve. The functions have already been written—you just need to understand when and how to employ them.

Part III, *Deployment and Continuous Delivery*, explains how to release your serverless applications into the world in a reliable, efficient, cost-effective, secure, testable manner that allows you to monitor their performance and continually improve them.

Who This Book Is For

This book is for experienced programmers who would like to familiarize themselves with functional programming through the lens of machine learning. As we said, the book uses Microsoft's Azure platform to build these systems, and it uses Python as the primary programming language.

Goals for the Book

When you are done with this book, we hope that you will be proficient in serverless programming in Azure as it relates to machine learning.

Using Python in Our Code Examples

Examples in this book are primarily in Python 3.6. Python is a widely used open source language, with runtimes, compilers, and tools available for all operating systems. It is well suited to use with the Azure platform. Python implements an object-oriented and functional paradigm and is one of the main languages used for machine learning projects, with many open source libraries available. All serverless platforms/providers support Python. You should be aware, however, that there are many other functional languages, for example JavaScript and Clojure, that are also well suited to this kind of programming.

If you know nothing about machine learning in Python, don't worry. We'll guide you through the core concepts, and the example code is meant to be short and supportive. If you find them difficult to fully understand, we encourage you to look for a short introductory Python course to get up to speed.

This book is here to help you get your job done. In general, if example code is offered in this book, you may use it in your programs and documentation. You do not need to contact us for permission unless you're reproducing a significant portion of the code. For example, writing a program that uses several chunks of code from this book does not require permission. Selling or distributing a CD-ROM of examples from O'Reilly books does require permission. Answering a question by citing this book and quoting example code does not require permission. Incorporating a significant amount of example code from this book into your product's documentation does require permission.

We appreciate, but do not require, attribution. An attribution usually includes the title, author, publisher, and ISBN. For example: "*Building Intelligent Cloud Applications* by Vicente Herrera García and John Biggs (O'Reilly). Copyright 2019 O'Reilly Media, Inc., 978-1-492-05221-0."

If you feel your use of code examples falls outside fair use or the permission given above, feel free to contact us at *permissions@oreilly.com*.

Conventions Used in This Book

The following typographical conventions are used in this book:

Italic
> Indicates new terms, URLs, email addresses, filenames, and file extensions.

`Constant width`
> Used for program listings, as well as within paragraphs to refer to program elements such as variable or function names, databases, data types, environment variables, statements, and keywords.

Constant width bold

Shows commands or other text that should be typed literally by the user.

Constant width italic

Shows text that should be replaced with user-supplied values or by values determined by context.

 This element signifies a tip or suggestion.

 This element signifies a general note.

 This element indicates a warning or caution.

O'Reilly Online Learning

 For almost 40 years, *O'Reilly Media* has provided technology and business training, knowledge, and insight to help companies succeed.

Our unique network of experts and innovators share their knowledge and expertise through books, articles, conferences, and our online learning platform. O'Reilly's online learning platform gives you on-demand access to live training courses, in-depth learning paths, interactive coding environments, and a vast collection of text and video from O'Reilly and 200+ other publishers. For more information, please visit *http://oreilly.com*.

How to Contact Us

Please address comments and questions concerning this book to the publisher:

O'Reilly Media, Inc.
1005 Gravenstein Highway North
Sebastopol, CA 95472
800-998-9938 (in the United States or Canada)
707-829-0515 (international or local)
707-829-0104 (fax)

To comment or ask technical questions about this book, send email to *bookquestions@oreilly.com*.

For more information about our books, courses, conferences, and news, see our website at *http://www.oreilly.com*.

Find us on Facebook: *http://facebook.com/oreilly*

Follow us on Twitter: *http://twitter.com/oreillymedia*

Watch us on YouTube: *http://www.youtube.com/oreillymedia*

## PART I

Cloud-Based Development

## CHAPTER 1

Machine Learning and Deep Learning Models in the Cloud

It doesn't seem that long ago that artificial intelligence (AI) was a dream. The idea that a machine could simulate and even beat humans at games of skill, image recognition, and predictions was preposterous 20 years ago. Now, the average user brushes up against some form of machine learning every day and everywhere—from our cars to stores to doctors' offices, and throughout our homes.

We are living at the dawn of thinking machines. But how do they think? What do they use to build models of the world? And how can we, as developers, use these tools to make our systems smarter, more responsive, and more lifelike?

Our goal in this book is to discuss the basics of machine learning and to show you, in a step-by-step introduction, how to implement and code machine learning into your projects using serverless systems and pretrained models. We can think of machine learning as a tool for interacting with an ever-changing world using models that change and grow as they experience more of that world. In other words, it's how we teach computers new things without explicitly programming them to do anything.

An Introduction to Machine Learning

The AI discipline, of which machine learning is a part, was born in the 1950s, during the Cold War, as a promise to develop systems that could solve complex problems. At that time, computers were not powerful enough for the task. Over the years, AI began to encompasses many different subdisciplines, from algorithms used to find a maze exit to systems that could recognize human emotions, drive cars, and predict future outcomes.

Machine learning, also often referred to as *ML*, is the study and creation of algorithms that become better at a specific task when they receive more data about that task. Most machine learning models begin with "training data" such as a large group of emails or a huge folder of images, which the machine processes and begins to "understand" statistically. Because machine learning assumes no active human programming, the machine algorithm itself changes and grows as it addresses the training data. After a while, the algorithm is ready for "real" data. It continues to evolve as it processes new information, ultimately leading to an answer or solution without outside intervention.

Machine learning is important for the simple reason that not all problems consist of a closed set of variables and routines. For example, a machine learning model could be tasked to analyze spots on the skin for cancer. Because every spot is different, the machine learning model will categorize each spot based on its own statistically chosen criteria and, when queried, will return its best guess as to whether a spot is cancerous—which, in many cases, is as good or better than a human guess. Traditional algorithms solve very specific, bounded problems. Machine learning lets us train a model to solve something that we initially might not know how to do.

We must also remember the difference between algorithms and training. You can have an algorithm for facial recognition that uses a set of training data passed into the system by the developer. But if your goal is something else—to look for vehicle license plates in pictures of cars, for example—you might use the same simple pattern recognition algorithm with the new dataset. Depending on your use case, you could either look for a model that has the algorithm and present new data on which to train it, or look for a model that's already trained for the problem that you are trying to solve.

Models aren't always perfect, however. Researcher Victoria Krakovna created a popular list of machine learning "mistakes" (*https://bit.ly/2RV1HOu*) in which the machine learned to achieve goals in ways that didn't address the problems that humans were trying to solve. In a life simulation game, for example, "creatures bred for jumping were evaluated on the height of the block that was originally closest to the ground. The creatures developed a long vertical pole and flipped over instead of jumping." Another foible appeared in the video game *Sims*, in which "creatures exploited physics simulation bugs by twitching, which accumulated simulator errors and allowed them to travel at unrealistic speeds." Our absolute favorite, however, involves the cannibalistic parents of another life simulation. As Krakovna describes:

> In an artificial life simulation where survival required energy but giving birth had no energy cost, one species evolved a sedentary lifestyle that consisted mostly of mating in order to produce new children which could be eaten (or used as mates to produce more edible children).

These comical examples—edible children?—point to the sometimes weird conclusions that machine learning systems make when looking at data that humans would find opaque. But we can't blame these machines for their will to "win." After all, that's all they're programmed to do!

Machine learning algorithms are very diverse, having many different models that we can use for solving problems like prediction of outcomes and estimation (in which some value fluctuates by some natural causes) and classification of elements (e.g., examining satellite pictures to determine which areas are urban, which are forests, and which are bodies of water).

Examples of machine learning algorithms include the following:

Anomaly detection
This can identify rare items, events, or observations that differ significantly from the majority of the data. It can be used to detect bank fraud, for example.

Classification
This is good for predicting the classes of given data points. It's useful, for example, in spam detection or identifying tumors.

Clustering
This groups a set of objects in such a way that objects in the same group are more similar in some sense to one another than to those in other groups. It is useful in pattern recognition, image analysis, data compression, biological classification, and insurance, for example.

Recommendation
Using a dataset of user-item-rating triples, this model can generate recommendations and find related items. It is used in media streaming services to recommend movies or music as well as online shops to recommend items to customers.

Regression
This is used to infer the expected quantity for an input related to a set of data points. Assuming that there is a linear, polinomic, logistic, or any other mathematical relation between inputs and outputs, the best coefficients possible of this math relation are inferred. Any type of experiment that records data uses this type of analysis to prove mathematical relation or correlation. In business, it's used to forecast revenue, and insurance companies rely on regression analysis to estimate credit standing of policy holders and possible number of claims in a given time period.

Statistical functions
Machine learning can compute mathematical operations over a large set of data. It can also calculate correlation and probability scores and compute z-scores, as well as statistical distributions such as Weibull, gamma, and beta. Statistics has many applications to understand and model systems with a large number of elements. Governments and other organizations use it to understand data pertain-

ing to wealth, income, crimes, and so on. Businesses use it to know what to produce and when. Social and natural scientists use it to study the demographic characteristics of a population.

Text analytics

This extracts information from text, such as most likely language used or key phrases. Sentiment analysis is an example application.

Computer vision

This is used to read text in images or handwritten notes, recognize human faces or landmarks, and analyze video in real time.

What these machine learning techniques all have in common is that they rely on learning automatically from a very large set of data. The programmer can define the algorithm architecture and some initial parameters, and then the program learns itself by studying the data.

If you want to know about what you can achieve with these techniques, here are some great examples of success stories for machine learning projects:

JFK Files

In 2017, more than 34,000 pages related to the assassination of John F. Kennedy were released by the United States government, consisting of a mixture of typed and handwritten documents. Thanks to Azure Search and Cognitive Services, a set of composable cognitive skills were applied to this data to extract knowledge and organize it into an index. Not only can this system answer many interesting questions, but you also see the answers and relationships in context with the original documents.

Snip Insights

This is an open source screen-capture desktop application that uses Azure Cognitive Services to gain instant insight into the image just captured. It can convert images to text and display information about the subject (for example, identifying celebrities and landmarks). If the image is of a product, the application will automatically search for similar products, providing information about how much each one costs and where to buy it.

Pix2Story

This is a web application that uses natural language processing (NLP) to teach an AI system, inspired by a picture, to write a machine-generated story. Captions obtained from the uploaded picture are fed to a recurrent neural network model to generate the narrative based on the genre and the contents of the picture.

Sketch2Code

This is an AI solution that converts hand-drawn renderings on paper or whiteboard to working HTML prototypes. After training the model with images of hand-drawn design elements like text boxes, buttons, or combo boxes, the Custom Vision Service performs object detection to generate the HTML snippets of each element.

To learn more about these and other examples, visit the Microsoft AI Lab website (*http://www.ailab.microsoft.com*).

An Introduction to Deep Learning

Deep learning is a class of machine learning algorithms that does the following:

- Uses a cascade of multiple layers of nonlinear processing units for feature extraction and transformation. Each successive layer uses the output from the previous layer as input.
- Learns in supervised (e.g., classification) and/or unsupervised (e.g., pattern analysis) ways.
- Learns multiple levels of representations that correspond to different levels of abstraction. The levels form a hierarchy of concepts.

Deep learning's use of this hierarchy of concepts and classifications contrasts with the often-brutish machine learning methods popular in the lab.

When we have many hidden layers in a model, we say that the network is a deep learning system because deep within the layers of the model it retains the knowledge it is gaining from the examples. We can use these kinds of models in a lot of groundbreaking applications thanks to the great processing power available in modern computers. But with each new layer of complexity, even more power is required to achieve new goals.

Neural Networks

The next frontier in machine learning is the neural network. The idea of the computer-based neural network has been around for decades, but only recently has hardware arrived with sufficient horsepower to make it widely useful. The neural network is built on a model of how a human brain works. We begin with a simple data processor called a *perceptron*, which works as a base neuron does in our own brains. Like a neuron, each perceptron takes an input, checks it against a gate function, and produces an output that can, at the same time, control other perceptrons. This net of perceptrons is called an *artificial neural network*, which you can see in Figure 1-1.

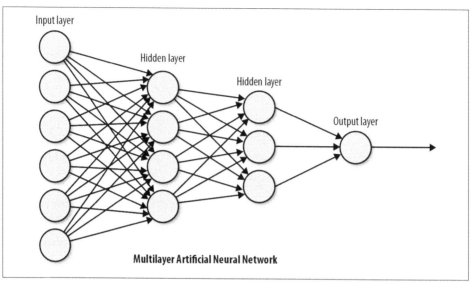

Figure 1-1. A neural network with two hidden layers

But how does this system learn? Whenever a perceptron gets a strong enough signal, it reinforces the weights of its input to the activation function, so it is easier to fire again on the same conditions. A simple multilayer neural network has an input layer of perceptrons, some hidden layers that accept input from previous ones and feed the next ones, and a final output layer. There can also be intermediate layers whose outputs serve as inputs for previous layers. In this way, active feedback is built into the system.

Difficulties Defining Structure and Training Machine Learning Models

Figure 1-2 illustrates that a deep learning neural model can have a very complex structure that can be properly created only by an expert. Also, as shown previously, the list of different machine learning models can be extensive, and understanding how you must tune the settings of each one for the kind of problem that you want to solve is no small task. As we discuss shortly, this is why you can benefit from using premade and pretrained models.

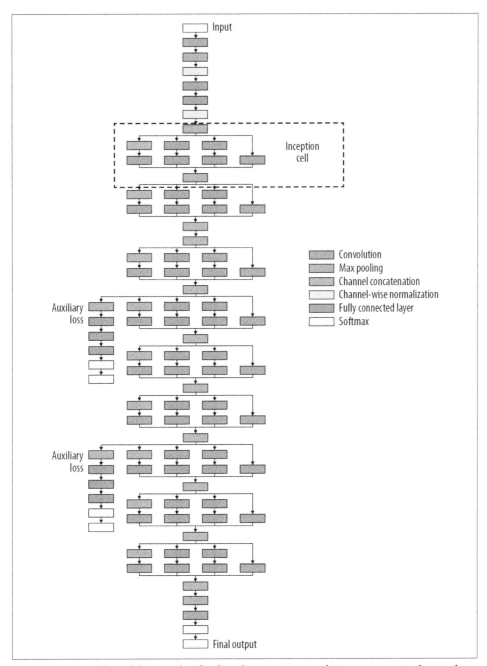

Figure 1-2. A real-world example of a deep learning network; its structure is the product of a lot of work to fine-tune how it operates.

The data you have for training must have not only input values, but also the output answer that you want the model to learn. When you have a fixed set of data to work on, it's important to separate it into training, validation, and test sets. Only the first one is used as to train the model, feeding all of its data to the learning process. Then you use the validation set, which the model has not seen, to ensure that it can do meaningful predictions. You use the trained model to process the validation data and compare the output that the data must yield with what the model inferred from it. If the model training has gone well, the output should be very accurate.

One of the problems that you must consider when working with machine learning models is *overfitting* to the training data. You want a model that is versatile and can make good predictions given new data that it hasn't seen before. If you overtrain your model with data that is very similar, it will lose the capacity to extrapolate to other cases. That is why the verification with separate data becomes important. Lastly, the test set has the real data you need to use to create a prediction. For this set, you don't know the real outcome until the model tells you what it is.

When models finish training, they are effectively "black boxes." It can be difficult or virtually impossible for humans to perceive the statistically based logic that a model is using to arrive at its answers. After a model has been trained and you get good output results, you can copy and use it again anywhere you want (provided the kind of data you are using is similar), but you can't analyze how the algorithm works to try to infer some kind of knowledge. The model will have made a large number of connections within itself using the data provided, and trying to understand it would be as difficult as trying to make the prediction about the data you are analyzing.

So, having lots of varied data is crucial for a well-trained model, and this means that training is going to require a great deal of computing power and is going to be time-consuming. Also, finding the right combination of model type and initial setup for a specific kind of problem can be very tricky, and you should always check the state of the art of the machine learning community for details on how to use the latest models for different types of problems.

An Introduction to Serverless Machine Learning

In this book, we talk about how serverless architectures can support the implementation of machine learning and deep learning workloads in the cloud. By taking advantage of a serverless machine learning service and passing it a set of data, we are able to offload a great deal of the work associated with training and analysis to platforms perfectly suited to the job.

The first benefit of serverless machine learning is that each machine you use is ready to run when needed and can be shut down immediately when it isn't needed. You can also very easily use models and algorithms that are already written and stored in a library instead of having to write code yourself to deploy on your machines. This saves both money and time.

In fact, using premade models makes more sense given that the number of cloud-based models that are available is very high. This means that there is often no reason to reinvent the wheel in machine learning: there is a constantly growing number of algorithm optimizations for supporting parallel computing, for using less memory, and for starting up, running, and shutting down quickly. In almost every case, if we run an experiment with the serverless model and use prewritten models, we're going to have a faster execution time. This is because the models are already optimized and fine-tuned with the best training possible for their task by experts, and the computer power a cloud provider can deliver yields greater performance than what we can achieve with our own infrastructure.

After we have decided on our model, another advantage of the serverless approach becomes apparent. If we were hosting a custom model on our own servers, we'd need to worry about scaling the system in a live environment. In a serverless architecture, this scaling is automatic. We will be charged for what we use, and the price is proportional to the workload.

Cloud providers like Amazon Web Services (AWS) and Microsoft Azure often allow serverless users to employ ready-made models including tools like image recognition, speech recognition, and object classification. In this case, you barely need to know anything about machine learning. Instead, you simply implement the model without having to think about *how* a certain image of a storefront returns metadata like the store's name and the products in the picture. It just works. Using prepopulated machine learning models is an easy way to begin doing things with machine learning —you need to understand only what you're trying to infer or detect.

Cloud providers have actually created a number of tools that solve common problems and don't even advertise themselves as machine learning. For example, Azure offers the Swiftly Speech to Text service that can transcribe input audio of someone speaking into text. It relies on a machine learning model already trained for speech recognition.

Equally importantly, cloud providers offer methods to enforce security and user access as well as billing and cost control. This means that you can chain models in ways that are unique to your use case and ensure a reduction of security failures or billing surprises.

Event-driven architectures are unique in that they run only when called. In a traditional server architecture, code sits idle on an idle machine until it is needed. The result is that you must pay for a server running constantly, even if the code it hosts isn't being run. In serverless, if a function is never called, there's no cost to you. This code, which is parceled into event-driven services, is very easy to write, and it's even easier to glue these functions together to create new functions. For example, you could build a function that takes as an input sound from an emergency phone call for an earthquake watch service, passes the sound to a machine learning model that transcribes it to text, and then forwards the text to an SMS sender service so that first responder personnel are notified. When everything is tied together, until you receive your first call, you pay nothing except for a little server space to store your code.

Using a serverless approach, the code is simple and clear because you don't need to add parts necessary to manage virtual machines (VMs) and other resource-intensive tasks. All of the difficult "sysadmin" stuff—VM provisioning and autoscaling, stopping inactive VMs, even security and monitoring—is handled by the cloud provider. You also get analytic services that help you to inspect the performance of the machine learning models and any other cloud provider features that you are using. If you are running a critical service, they show you graphs with all the parameters that you want to measure without you having to insert this code into your functions. The analytics are baked in.

Although there is theoretically no limit to the kind of work that you can manage in a serverless application, there are some restrictions that you need to take into consideration. For example, Azure offers a maximum of 10 minutes per function call. If your function runs longer than that, Azure dumps the process. Azure assumes that functions should be very quick and that your function can call another function in series. This architectural philosophy assumes that if your function lasts more than 10 minutes, something is very wrong.

Using Containers with Machine Learning Models

Having pretrained machine learning models is very useful, and a serverless architecture ensures that you can scale effortlessly. But given that this area of technology advances quickly, you might find that you not only need to use custom models but also might need to design your own architecture.

In this case, you can work with *containers*, which are similar to VMs but a lot "lighter." Using containers, any parameter that is not defined by you is still managed by the cloud provider. The behavior of containers is predictable, repeatable, and *immutable*. This means that there are no unexpected errors when you move them to a new machine, or between environments. You can then create a cluster of containers with a configuration suited to your machine learning requirements. Having a cloud provider that provides the means to easily coordinate (or "orchestrate") these containers and to monitor and scale them in a way that is "as serverless as possible" is a great advantage. Working this way, you can have the best of both worlds: an almost serverless approach and, at the same time, customization of your containers to best suit your needs.

Right now, the state of the art for container orchestration is *Kubernetes*, an open source solution that some cloud providers offer. It manages for you the resources of different nodes (physical machines). On each one, it deploys one or more *kubelets*, which are sets of containers that need to work together. It then scales the number of kubelets up or down automatically to satisfy the requirements of the incoming load.

Figure 1-3 depicts an example architecture for managing a containerized application (one that uses containers) with Kubernetes. It is a little complex, but the magic about it is that, again, you don't need to understand all of the details. You just prepare your containers on your own machine (which we explain in the examples), upload them to the Kubernetes Service cloud provider, and leave the difficult work to them.

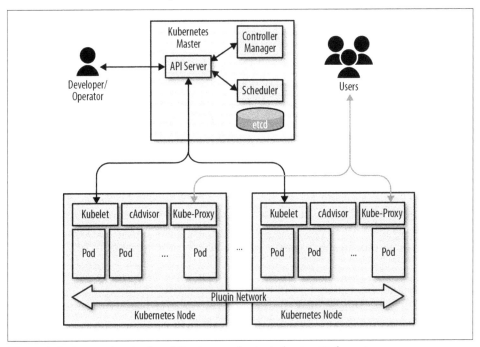

Figure 1-3. A containerized architecture orchestrated using Kubernetes

The Benefits of Serverless Computing for Machine Learning

To summarize our argument so far, serverless computing in machine learning has many benefits, including the following:

Infrastructure savings

This is a no-brainer. Without a server, you pay nothing for your own servers. This doesn't mean Functions-as-a-Service (FaaS) is free. Instead, suppliers can be far more granular with their billing and charge you only for the code that you run. In turn, providers save resources by ensuring functions fire only as needed, thereby reducing operating overhead. Further, this infrastructure is someone else's problem. Your downtime doesn't depend on your code.

Code runs independently

Each piece of code in a serverless product is run independently. The spell-checking service doesn't need to interact with the math service; likewise, the address lookup service doesn't need to interact with the input services. We like to imagine this environment as a set of firecrackers shooting off in different parts of an empty room. The only entangling aspect is the initial match.

Scalability

As we noted before, this model ensures that VMs are powered down until needed. Because we are using an event-driven paradigm, these events trigger active code only as needed and remove the need for constant pooling—a problem that can grow as the project grows—and interdependencies that can slow down traditional programming projects. Functions can react to anything, be it vast amounts of telemetry, data, logs, sensor data, real-time streaming, and so on, and the system processes each chunk of data in parallel with no interaction with other parts of the machine.

Ease of training

Trigger-based functions are excellent for training machine learning applications. By sending massive amounts of training data to a set of virtualized functions we reduce the need for always-on training and can instead train and consume using virtual functions. In other words, FaaS makes for a solid set of machine learning tools.

In the next chapters, we explore how to build serverless architectures and use pre-made machine learning models in our projects. We also begin to demonstrate the depth and breadth of these robust models. Get ready to build!

## CHAPTER 2

Functions-as-a-Service and Event-Driven Programming

"People think that computer science is the art of geniuses, but the actual reality is the opposite, just many people doing things that build on each other, like a wall of mini stones," said computer science pioneer Donald Knuth. Nowhere is that more apparent than in the rise of cloud computing. In this chapter, we explore the expansion of functions from the "mini stones" of a program into a distributed and powerful system for scaling services up and down in a constantly changing environment. We also explore Functions-as-a-Service and event-driven programming—concepts necessary for putting these new computing paradigms into practice.

Software-as-a-Service, Cloud Computing, and Serverless

Before the internet, the traditional way of commercializing software was to sell an executable copy of it that you installed on your computer or server. When the internet made it possible to have almost any enterprise connected to a vast store of data and programs, another way of selling software products was born. Instead of buying shrink-wrapped software to install on your machines, you simply connected to a server operated by the software vendor, performed your work, and logged off. For vendors, the Software-as-a-Service (SaaS) model had many advantages: they could charge by usage, it was easy to update their servers, and it rendered software piracy impossible. There were complementary benefits for software consumers: they didn't need to worry about owning and operating their own computers, maintenance headaches were taken care of by the vendor, and so forth.

When SaaS offers an application programming interface (API) that defines how to interconnect to this system from others, it is said to have a *service-oriented architecture* (SOA), because it can be thought of as a set of services that can be evoked programmatically.

The next step in this architectural evolution brought us the idea that every aspect of infrastructure and operations could be handled automatically, "from provisioning and setting up virtual servers [to] scaling, configuration, security, and backups." This approach, pioneered by the team at Fotango in 2005, assumed that users wanted no truck with the command line. Rather than spin up a virtual server, install files, and hope everything runs when you're done, it said that all of that—from the server to the command to run the program—could be abstracted out and controlled by a vendor that could bill down to the function call.

This idea, known as *serverless computing*, is a game changer for many programmers, and it is vitally important to us in this book.

But as this model became increasingly popular, service providers allocated more resources to meet the incoming demand for services. This meant more machines, more developers, and more work. Over time another way to increase efficiency arose that left the "dirty work" such as server maintenance, installation, and uptime monitoring to a specialized third party, which not only maintains servers but offers them in virtualized versions. Figure 2-1 demonstrates the difference. As it shows, these "virtual machines" ran on real hardware, but you didn't need to own or maintain it. When hardware needed to be replaced, your VM could be swapped to a different piece of hardware without you or your customers ever noticing.

In a serverless context, you don't need to worry about space for your hardware, monitoring, or replacing faulty equipment. But you still need to provision additional VMs when the workload grows larger, and shut some VMs down when the load falls.

Serverless is important when dealing with an irregular flow of processing data. Imagine, for example, an online Christmas website that is flush with visitors buying things in December but whose traffic is nearly nonexistent during the rest of the year. During these lulls the server still runs at full speed and uses all of the same resources it needed during the Christmas season.

With serverless, that changes considerably.

A serverless solution starts by detecting your current load and estimating future need. With a bit of tweaking, you can easily predict Christmas demand or even spikes for Black Friday, Easter Monday, or any other permutation. As the server runs, however, imagine that your store one day finds itself featured in the *New York Times*. Suddenly, it receives a deluge of visits—possibly millions. Serverless autoscaling is exactly the trick to ensure that your site doesn't fail immediately after the first few dozen visitors check out.

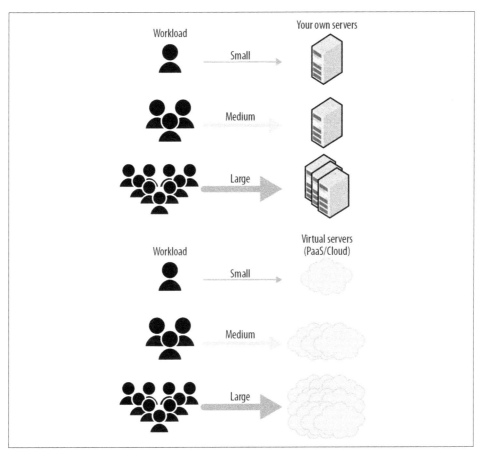

Figure 2-1. A simple approximation of working with different workloads when you build your own infrastructure and when you use a cloud service provider

Before cloud providers offered serverless solutions, you needed multiple copies of the same service, each one waiting in hibernation until called into use by rising demand. With the addition of each server, you needed to stop work, copy all of the data over to the new server, and hope that no one was checking out during that agonizing process. Thanks to all of this sudden interest, you'd enjoy a solid few hours of rapid-fire commerce and constant updates to your various servers. Then, at the end of the day, all of that traffic would go away. Again, with previous architectures this meant that your new servers would now be idle until the monitors realized what had happened. And if the lull in traffic was a fluke, these waiting servers could spin down and then need to spin up again as soon as new users returned.

Years of effort have allowed users to fine-tune this process, but it is clear that a serverless scenario is far superior.

Microservices Architecture

How programs organize code is important in an attempt to solve increasingly difficult challenges to satisfy complex requirements. For example, imagine a small application like a simple online music service that grows to offer shared playlists, related music, social media integration, and the ability to share what you are listening to with your friends. If more code is added with no organization, you end up with a mess in which a lot of things depend on one another, and it's difficult to make changes without incurring many errors. To assure that the code can adapt to changes, evolve, and be resilient to problems in execution, several program architectures have arisen for organizing code that runs on computers.

One of these approaches is *microservices*, which consists of dividing your program into small systems that each take an input and return an output. Defined first by Dr. Peter Rogers during a conference on cloud computing in 2005, in 2011 the term was applied at an event for software architects by a group of solutions developers who were already starting to use it, and it was then popularized by the likes of Netflix, Amazon, and Spotify.

Before microservices, a project would usually consist of a single, large executable that could perform several tasks and offer many services. Developers called this the *monolithic approach*. But all of the parts would be highly related, and an update for your customers would require deploying a new executable. Also, if something in the program failed in a critical way, the entire application would crash and no services would run.

The microservices architecture solves these problems by splitting projects into many small parts, each of them a project on its own. These microservices communicate among one another and work in a coordinated manner to bring services to your customers using the same protocols and standards that your customers use to communicate with your services. Figure 2-2 demonstrates how microservices serve functionality from several small applications at the same time rather than from one application. This way, you don't need to have knowledge of the entire body of code in the project to update functionality; you can update just one microservice at a time. You can deploy new functionality by creating a new microservice that communicates with the other ones. And, more importantly, if one microservice fails, the rest continue to run.

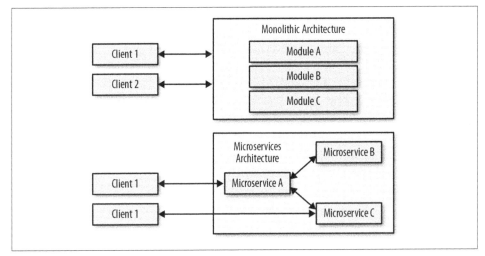

Figure 2-2. How external clients connect to a monolithic and a microservices architecture

The value of these microservices comes in their variety and power. For example, a microservice might return GPS data, or an analysis of a scene, or turn speech into text. Further, you can very easily transform a free microservice into a paid microservice, something the blockchain startup called 21 attempted at around the same time as the launch of Hook (*https://hook.io*).

In other words, these microservices are actually functions in disguise and hosted on other servers. Thanks to cryptocurrency and other payment tools, you can send micropayments for your microservices, a fun and lucrative addition to the programmer's arsenal.

All of these new developments are made possible by a class of programming languages that are called *functional*. Let's take a closer look at this.

The Rise of Functional Programming

The *functional programming* paradigm has been around for some time. It has its origin in the mathematical Lambda calculus, a formal system developed in the 1930s to describe functions. This formal system was used as the basis for many computer programming languages, notably LISP, which abstracted many operations. Proponents of functional programming said that it made it easy to manage complexity and was inherently more powerful and flexible than other approaches. But many programmers found it difficult to grasp the functional way of thinking, and such programs were often big (taking longer to compile) and slow. For a long time, functional programming remained a niche art. Then, as computers became more and more powerful, this began to change.

Until recently, object-oriented programming (OOP), a different paradigm than functional programming, was far more popular. Object orientation brought us a robust model on which all graphical user interfaces (GUIs) are built and has many important benefits in and of itself. But with the rise of the internet, and what came to be called *web 2.0*, browsers became a crucial tool with which to build functionality—and the key programming language for web development, JavaScript, relies on a functional programming paradigm. That made this paradigm popular, and people working with it became more skilled with time.

At first JavaScript was used only for simple things like hiding and showing or moving elements of a web page. But later, full-fledged complex programs, such as webmail clients, that run completely within the browser were developed in JavaScript. Complex data structures were handled in JavaScript, as well as asynchronous communication between client and server. Eventually, JavaScript also became popular for backend development on the servers that feed the web pages, and *Node.js* was born. As an example of the "mini stones" that together build a great wall, many frameworks, libraries, and algorithms have been built upon the functional programming paradigm, and many programming languages that were not based on functional programming have been modified to enable that way of coding so that they can be used in this way.

In essence, functional programming is very similar to subroutines in pure imperative and procedural languages (e.g., Pascal, Fortran, or Basic) and to the invocation of static methods found in object-oriented languages like C++, Java, or early versions of C#. What's unique about functional programming is that within *pure functions*, no side effects can occur. In procedural languages, information is shared among different parts of the program by means of variables that can be read and modified. In purely functional languages it is impossible to do this.

This means that to remain "pure," the functions cannot create any files or store any data. The only change they create is in the output of the function. This simple statement not only makes it easier to understand what functions can do, but also makes it clear why functions are then more appropriate for parallel execution. Now, it becomes apparent that functional programming requires new ways of thinking about algorithms. Even though obviously anything in computing exhibits this sort of behavior—it wouldn't do for a machine to give a different answer to the same question two times in a row—it can be challenging for programmers accustomed to languages like C or C++ to come up with an application structure using only functions (oddly enough, because object orientation and procedural programming scripting offer some messy ways of thinking about inputs and outputs). Functions are very easy to code and understand, as you can see in the example code that follows, but learning that level of simplicity in order to incorporate them into complex software architecture can be surprisingly difficult:

```
def my_function(a, b):
    return a+b
# Execute
print(my_function(3,2))
```

Remember that in functional programming you can pass functions as input or output parameters of other functions. The next code example shows a function used as a parameter in this way. We create an array of numbers, and then we create a function that returns the power of two of a number supplied as input to the function. Then, we use both the squaring function (sqr) and the array as inputs to another function, called map, that iterates over each element of the array and applies the squaring function to it.

The second part of the code example does the same thing as the first block, but using the technique of an unnamed (or anonymous, or nameless) function. In it, we don't even give a name to the function, using instead the language keyword lambda. We can use the same technique when we pass a literal number or a string to a function call, without storing it first in a variable:

```
# Python already has a map function, but we will define it here for our purposes
def map(myfunction, myarray):
    for e in myarray:
        e = myfunction(e)
# We define an array, and a function sqr
s = [1, 3, 5, 7, 9]
def sqr(x):
    return x ** 2
# We pass both to the map function to apply to each element
map(sqr, s)
print(s)

# Same thing, but we do not name the input function (using lambda)
s = [1, 3, 5, 7, 9]
map((lambda x: x**2), s)
print(s)
```

Many programmers who are used to OOP are used to thinking about *classes* of objects and *instances* of objects, for example. These objects have methods that are similar to functions, but when you execute an object's method, it can return different outputs depending on the different states in which the object can be. For example, if you have an object that represents the arm of a robot that you have in a factory, and you make a call to a method to ask the object to move completely to the left, the posi tion property of the object is going to change. If you again call this method with the same input, it could well return an error, because the arm has already moved to its maximum position. In the following example, we have a simple example of object-oriented code in Python 3 for a class that defines RobotArm and its position state:

```
class RobotArm:
    # Class attribute
    type = 'Robotic Arm'
    # Initializer /
    def __init__(self, name, position):
        self.name = name          # Instance attributes
        self.position = position

    def turn(self, distance):
        self.position = self.position + distance
        return (self.position)
    def print_position(self):
        print("position {}.".format(self.position))

# Execute
arm = RobotArm("T100", 5)
arm.turn(2)
arm.print_position()
arm.turn(-5)
arm.print_position()
arm.turn(2)
arm.print_position()
```

The position of the arm lives in the state of the object. That's very useful from the object-oriented paradigm point of view because everything about that real-life object is encapsulated in such a way that you don't need to know what is inside it. You need to know only the methods to perform actions on the object. But anyone who has built a complex object-oriented project knows that scaling is a serious issue. When you want to scale operations to several nodes running code at the same time, it's very difficult to synchronize the state for an object in each node and send messages when it changes. You begin to see a massive reduction in speed and an increase in complexity.

Using Functions Instead of Objects

How can we accommodate this in functional programming? We need to store a state somewhere outside of the function and pass it as an input. Do you want to close the open hand of the arm? Run a function with *state* and *close operation* as input parameters, and receive new state as an output. Want to open the hand? Run another function and again pass the current state. That way, because functions know nothing but what is sent to them, many instances of the same code can be hosted on different servers at the same time. A call to a function will return the same state given the same input without fail, no matter what server is hosting it. If a different state is passed to the function, we'll get a different result.

We have explained that the best way to achieve scalability and resilience in your applications is to use pure functions whenever possible. But side effects are necessary because if data is not read from somewhere or it is not saved somewhere else, our program is going to be of little use. The way to solve this problem is to isolate input/

output operations in specialized functions and use other pure functions to perform transformations, calculations, or processing activities. An example of how to achieve that could be something like that shown in the code that follows, in which we try to achieve a similar result as when we were using a class. We must pass the arm variable state to each function. This way, we isolate pure functions (turn) and input/output functions (print_position):

```
def turn(armState, distance):
 armState['position'] = armState['position'] + distance
 return armState
def print_position(armState):
 print("position {}."format(armState['position']))
# Execute
arm = {
 'type': 'Robotic Arm',
 'name': 'T100',
 'position': 0
}
arm['position'] = 5
arm = turn(arm, 2)
print_position(arm)
arm = turn(arm, -5)
print_position(arm)
arm = turn(arm, 2)
print_position(arm)
```

If we want to use pure functions, instead of having an object arm of class RobotArm with a method turn, we should have a pure function state, to which we pass the state of the robotic arm. This way, with the same input (state and distance for turning), we should always obtain the same output, and we have a pure function.

This stark code—passing single numbers to a function over and over—seems like it might be inefficient. However, in many situations, you could use this methodology to send multiple state changes to a function at once, ensuring that each one is done in turn and without slowing down the machine.

When your application begins to become larger, you should divide it into different parts that communicate with one another, following a microservices architecture. Functions in each microservice will be run in response to some kind of event. The output can trigger new events so that it also follows an event-driven programming approach.

Still concerned about functional programming? Well, don't be. You've been using functional systems for years. Almost all modern programming languages now have functional components because functional programming has proven to be very useful in a lot of situations. Every popular programming language—including C#, Java-Script, PHP, and Python—implements the functional programming paradigm.

There are also specialized programming languages like Clojure, Haskell, and Scala that are based solely on functional programming and constitute a purer way of employing this paradigm. They have been used for many important achievements, like orchestration of resources for telecommunications and financial analysis at Credit Suisse, Ericsson, and Nortel, as well as in many general applications at companies like Facebook, Yahoo!, and Amazon. They are the main reason that all the other programming languages have also been modified to be able to allow functional programming.

Asynchronous Programming

As a simple example we can have a function f that has two inputs, input1 and input2, and produces an output:

```
f(input1, input2) → output
```

But because functions can also be input or output parameters, we also can have a function f that accepts as inputs two other functions, fok and ferror:

```
f(input1, input2, fok, ferror) → output
```

Programming languages like JavaScript that implement the functional programming paradigm usually also enable *asynchronous programming*. In the preceding example, the function f could need to do a query to an external API that takes quite some time to answer. Using asynchronous programming, instead of waiting idle for the API to respond, you can let the program continue running while waiting for the API's response in a new computing thread. Then, when the query is answered, if it was successful, you execute the code in the fok function; if it wasn't successful, you execute the code in the ferror function.

In JavaScript this can be represented as follows:

```
makecall(input1, input2, function() {
    // OK
}, function() {
    // Error
});
```

Additionally, we can take into consideration the improvements of the language incorporated in the ECMAScript 2015 specification, as demonstrated in this example:

```
makecall(input1, input2).then((value) => {
    // OK
}, (reason) => {
    // Error
});
```

This kind of asynchronous programming is often associated with functional programming, but, as you can see, if the execution of the makecall function is launching a new thread and doing something in parallel with the execution of the main thread, it has some kind of side effect. Asynchronous calls are not pure functions but are essential in functional programming languages for managing I/O operations like writing to a file or reading data from an external point. They enable parallelization for these operations in separate threads, the same concept that we want to achieve with pure functions.

We should always separate functions that connect to an external source for input or output from those that adapt and process the data in transit. With this simple concept, we should gain a very high level of scalability and get the most out of the serverless infrastructure. We then say that those functions are *stateless* because they have no informational state, so each time they are executed, their output depends only on the values of the input. Each execution with the same input will always yield the same output.

For example, if you need to read temperature data from a database, transform it from Fahrenheit to Celsius scale (a simple math operation), and then write the result to a comma-separated values (CSV) file, the best approach would be this:

- Write a function to read from the database.
- Write another one that takes a value in Fahrenheit and transforms it and returns it as Celsius.
- Write a third one that takes that value as input and writes it to the CSV file.

This way, the data transformation function in the middle is a pure function and very easy to scale. In a more complex scenario, it instead could be a cognitive service that processes an input and returns its output.

Serverless

We have talked about microservices, functional programming, and cloud computing/ Platform-as-a-Service (PaaS). But what is their link? When we were discussing the serverless approach, we explained that although it relieves you from most of the burden of managing servers, you still must plan how you are going to launch more VMs when more load comes to your services. The difficult part here is that you need to know when to launch additional VMs and when to stop them. Synchronizing their work can be difficult if the architecture of your project has many interdependencies (not microservices-based).

Using functional programming, cloud providers now completely abstract all the VM management from you and instead offer a suite of functions. This is also known as Functions-as-a-Service (FaaS). Technically, FaaS is a kind of serverless because the underlying platform still is managed for you by your provider. As shown in

Figure 2-3, you don't need to know or care what happens inside the FaaS provider, only that you are charged for the service in proportion to how you use it.

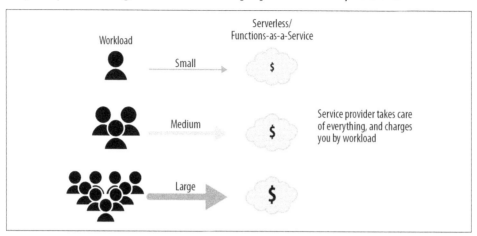

Figure 2-3. A simple representation of the implications of having different workloads on a serverless cloud provider

FaaS assumes a number of things about the functions in question. First, it's assumed that you are putting modular functions into a cloud service. This means that given a set of inputs, the outputs will always be the same.

Next, the system executes each function independently. This means that functions don't interact with or know about one another except when taking input values and returning output values. A function should not need to communicate with other functions if they are not part of its input to do its job. That is what enables the cloud provider to easily scale the work of functions: you can allocate more computers to run functions under the hood when there is a lot of work to process if you just give them their input and then read out their output.

FaaS also assumes that these functions store no data in the form of variables. Each instance produces a fresh, completely new instance with no connection to any other instance. This allows you to scale up quickly and easily by throwing new data at the same independent function and spinning up new servers as necessary, depending on the server load.

This does not mean that these services are completely dumb to the world. As they wink in and out of existence, they store data in distributed databases and can perform work that depends on this data. For example, if a function requires a sum of numbers that are supplied by all of the other functions running at the same time—a running tally, for example—the database can manage this with another function. A program then could request the total number of hits per day, and another function could easily poll the database or logs for that information without having to store any of it itself.

This is one of the primary benefits of FaaS. As a programmer, you don't design your code with servers in mind. If you're used to developing cloud-based applications, you might divide the work between two machines, and when you want to run code, you need to ask a cloud service provider to spin up an entirely new service. Further, if you build for just one machine, you are limited in terms of memory and processing power. Even given the advances in distributed technology, many programs aren't optimized for expansion over multiple machines. In short, many earlier programs are unable to scale sanely in practice (or in theory), and this has caused untold headaches as nonoptimized code encountered real-world traffic.

In contrast, provisioning serverless functions works well with microservices. Functions as isolated input/output units are almost nanoservices in and of themselves. Using them for building microservices architectures is extremely easy.

The best thing about FaaS for a developer is that your only parameter is your code. This code runs on one machine or it runs on thousands, and each function receives its own monitor, allowing you to pay for only the code that is run. The cloud provider, then, worries about starting machines, stopping machines, and predicting traffic based on previous experiences. In this case, the name "serverless" doesn't mean that there are no servers. There are indeed servers, but they are the provider's problem.

Theoretically, this gives the developer absolute power—something most developers enjoy. Whether you are sending one request or a million, the provider must keep up and ensure that all of your functions (*not* your servers) are constantly running. The moment you deploy these services, the provider begins to run your code and must solve a number of problems that you never need to worry about, including load balancing, time limits, and downtime.

If you start Microsoft Word on your home computer, you will have Word open at all times until you stop it. This means that, in theory, Word will be waiting to spell check, format, and paginate even when you have no intention of doing those things. Microsoft Word is a very big, monolithic program, and each component of the program knows a lot of things about all of the other components. These relationships are wildly difficult to separate in any real sense at this point in Word's development, and this model—the FaaS model—would be almost impossible to implement without rewriting the entire program from scratch.

This is why developers who are starting down the functional path should begin looking at functions in a very granular and disconnected way. That's a good thing. Functions that are stateless are far simpler and scale very well. In the case of serverless computing, all of the functions that you have written are asleep until an event arises that calls one of the functions into action—and then the next one, and the next one after that. When the functions do their jobs, they might call other services and functions, or, when they are finished, they can just go to sleep.

Further, the FaaS provider might have a number of pieces of code that you need to know nothing about. This code will wake up other functions in the toolchain, run your requests, and then shut down. But everything in this case is run by events, and these events stop when the processing stops. In fact, FaaS encourages efficiency by its very nature. Simplicity is vitally important, and by thinking in terms of simple functions chained together and then destroyed after use, we begin to create more and more granular programming habits.

Another example of FaaS thinking involves "liking" a post on social media. Suppose, for example, that you want to show these "likes" to every user. So, your website calls the server function that calculates the likes, passes out the results, and then falls asleep until someone else calls it. On the surface, this seems to be the same sort of technology already available. However, in FaaS, the function lies fully dormant. Further, when the function receives thousands of calls, it can reduce itself to a simple HTTP request—hit a URL, return a number. The reduction of functions to their barest essentials creates an environment of absolute simplicity.

The function has neither state nor prior knowledge. When you request the number of likes, the function single-mindedly goes about the task of gathering that data and sending it back without requiring any storage. When an event call comes down the wire, the event pulls all of the data necessary for the function to do its job. This doesn't mean that it's a black box. If you are calculating "likes" you will need to ask the database about the number of likes gathered thus far. But this process is instantaneous, and clever database design can reduce the execution time even further. Although the function holds no data, the database can be a bit smarter and know when to expect data output via stored procedures or other similar functions.

Again, the function knows nothing about its prior execution or the execution coming a moment later. It's a complete amnesiac and forgets everything. It knows nothing that it is not told by the user or the data store when its event is triggered. In this way, you can ensure that you can run many instances of the same function in parallel with no problems.

Implementing Functions

When it's time to begin coding some of these functions, you must first remember that functions are fluid. You can remove them, add them, and change them at will. As long as they accept the same inputs, and output the same types of outputs, they are interchangeable.

That having been said, every program needs a set of startup procedures. These procedures are the ones that tell what functions must be executed, and when.

For example, when some HTTP call is made from a browser, it can launch some function that processes its input data. We say that an HTTP request event triggers the execution of the function. Or we can have a database and, when some data record is changed, also trigger a data-change event and the execution of another function, that takes the modified data as an input. So we could have multiple executions. First, an HTTP request triggers a function, that writes to the database, and this again triggers another function that detects the change and also does something with the modified data.

For a more detailed example, maybe there's an event in the database that produces a list of users, and you have a function that changes the state of a user. Thus, that user state change that we detected runs a function that triggers a notification via a mobile application. These functions are easy to code. They just receive the user data, check its state, and if it is changed, call another function for the notification to be sent.

This approach also works well in the world of file storage. You can create a set of files or blocks and send and receive files via a website. You then can set up an event that triggers when a certain type of file is written. If an image ends up in that folder, an event can trigger a function to add cat ears to any faces it finds or, in more practical terms, it can begin learning about faces using a machine learning function.

In a real example, we might find ourselves looking for specific items within pictures; for example, a table with a specific type of leg and foot. This kind of task is important because it is difficult—discerning parts of a table in a scene is a tough task—and by training a network to recognize these things, we can use that model in other apps.

Event-Driven Architecture

Looking more closely at our previous example, when we upload a picture of a table, a chain of events is launched in the database, and it returns a notification that an image of a table has been uploaded. We use this framework to write machine learning models because we don't need to write much code. The code needed for this function is quite simply an upload processor, a function that looks for tables, and a notifier.

This is the basis for *event-driven architecture*, another organizational pattern that is very important for functional programming. In it, functions are always invoked by some kind of event, which contains a context with information about how the event was fired. Any number of event processors—in this case, functions—can respond to an event, process information, and also send new events to which other functions can respond. Not only that, but any other service offered by the cloud provider can be a source of events, like the database detecting a change of data or a file store reacting to a new file being created.

This kind of coordination paradigm is perfect for consuming complex functionality that your cloud provider offers you, using functional programming as glue to tie everything together. This results in environments in which little custom code is needed, where scaling is relatively easy, and where existing complex features can be reused. Figure 2-4 shows that without event-driven architecture, there is a lot of coupling, or dependence, between each part of the application, but with events it's easier to manage all of the functions that you add to the application.

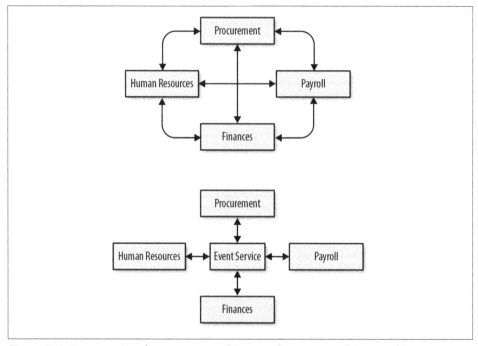

Figure 2-4. A comparison between event-driven and non-event-driven architecture

Building code that executes and operates in an event-driven way lets you build tools that can react to anything. This means that you can connect a learning system to a web page or a set of very fast sensors spread over a wide geographical region. Interestingly, you can build hardware that is event driven and that activates only when it reaches a certain threshold. This, in turn, saves on battery life and ensures that only applicable data gets to the reader when certain levels are met.

Sporadic data isn't the only form usable by this system. A hospital, for example, might send massive amounts of medical data via a monitoring system and look only for subtle changes in the data feed. Because each function is separate, this requires very little computing power and instead necessitates only a quick hit to a database to check for anomalous data.

Implications of Real-Time Processing

All of these implementations are far easier in a serverless scenario. Before these paradigms took hold, developers could store only chunks of data and then analyze it offline. Suppose, for example, that you want to analyze a year's worth of data in retrospect. With a server-based architecture, all of that data enters the system in series and is processed a chunk at a time. With serverless architectures, you can split the data among millions of nodes that can analyze it all at once. This allows you to check for anomalies in real time.

Let's look again at our hospital example. By analyzing all of the patient data at once, we are able to pinpoint times when the patient's medical status changed and understand what happened before and after that particular situation arose. This, in turn, gives us a methodology to predict similar behaviors in the patient (or in another application, the stock market, or weather sensors) to extrapolate expected behavior, given a massive set of changing variables.

Enabling machine learning in this way ensures an exponential progression versus a linear one. Because many data points can be consumed at once, we aren't afraid of vast oceans of data in cold storage or freshly minted by telemetry data or sensor inputs. Machine learning models in this architecture can help a lot because they see everything, they learn from everything, and we don't need to understand what's happening inside of the functions to use them. In short, we can feed all of this information to the models to make predictions using chunks of code that are run in parallel in the most efficient ways possible. Figure 2-5 illustrates how your function's code now is the glue that chains the flow of data between these modules.

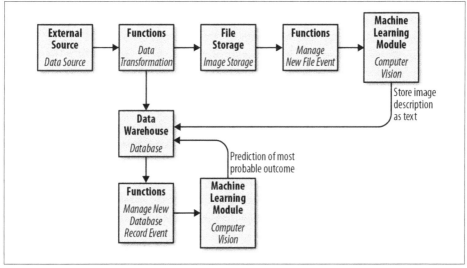

Figure 2-5. A simplified example of a machine learning serverless event-driven architecture

Summary and Look Ahead

In this chapter as well as Chapter 1, we have given an overview of cloud and server-less infrastructure, machine learning and deep learning systems, functional programming, and general software architecture. For each of these fields, we've barely scratched the surface. We encourage you to investigate further because there are a lot of topics to delve into.

In the following chapters, we continue with a more detailed and practical approach to serverless and intelligent serverless applications, using Azure to build working systems.

## CHAPTER 3

Serverless Application Programming Interfaces in Microsoft Azure

As we noted in Chapters 1 and 2, a serverless environment might be as beneficial for the cloud provider as it is for the developer. It is good for the provider because it is a way to ensure that its machines are always working on real tasks and not sitting idle, and it's good for developers because they don't need to think about server management. Now we introduce another concept, the idea of the *application programming interface* (API) as a way to access the many objects, methods, and functions available on the Azure platform.

APIs in Serverless Platforms

An API is how one program communicates with other programs. If you are going to build serverless machine learning solutions, cloud providers can accommodate your code in any of several programming languages. But you also must consider what serverless APIs these providers offer.

When you deploy your serverless code, it must interface with other services to do meaningful work. You will need, for example, to read and write data from databases and filesystems. But there are also many other services at your disposal, from pretrained machine learning modules to services for ingesting data from Internet of Things (IoT) devices, coordinating and communicating events, managing security, and exposing your own APIs.

The first step is to choose one serverless cloud provider and explore the different serverless APIs that it offers. There are several cloud providers for serverless applications that also offer machine learning services to interface with your programs. In this book, we'll work with *Azure Functions*, the serverless cloud service provided by

Microsoft. But if you prefer to choose a different provider, the core concepts, theoretical knowledge, and problem-solving abilities we present are going to be the same, and you shouldn't have any problem applying them on other microservice platforms.

An Introduction to Azure

Of all the cloud providers available, why choose Azure? There are many good reasons. Remember the old Microsoft and how it tied everything into its Windows operating systems? That has changed. A lot. All of the tools involved in Azure—.NET Core and Functions Core Tools—are open sourced, and the company now makes a serious effort to ensure that they are available and work on any operating system.

The serverless framework that Azure uses to execute your code is not a black box, but an environment that you can install on any computer to develop, test, and debug your serverless program. The first programming language that was available for Azure Functions was C#, but you can now use them with many others, including JavaScript (Node.js), Python, Java, F#, and PowerShell. More are coming, too.

Something that sets Azure apart from other providers is the *Azure Portal*. Here, you will find powerful DevOps tools that you can use to build an integrated delivery pipeline to do the following:

- Automate deployment of new versions of your code.
- Store your code in a source control framework.
- Access unit and integration testing to ensure that new versions of your applications, when they need to go live, are tested and ready to be used.

You can also quickly switch from a Consumption plan to an App Service plan pricing model, which takes away the pay-per-execution model.

The Azure Portal provides many integrated tools for security, disaster recovery, redundancy, availability, and scalability. It is a very cost-effective solution that offers several free services for the first year (see Table 3-1) and many other services that are always free (Table 3-2). You can rest easy knowing that one million function calls are always free, and you won't be charged for any call that yields an error status of 500 or 404 Not Found. You can find more information on creating an account (*https:// azure.microsoft.com/en-us/free/*), estimating your future costs (*https://azure.micro soft.com/en-us/pricing/calculator/*), and using Azure billing to control your costs and prevent unexpected charges (*https://docs.microsoft.com/en-us/azure/billing/billing-getting-started*) on the Azure website.

Table 3-1. *Azure products that are free for 12 months*

Product	Usage limit
Linux VM	750 hours
Windows VM	750 hours
Managed Disks	64 GB x 2
Blob Storage	5 GB
SQL Database	5 GB
Cosmos DB	5 GB
Data Transfer	15 GB

Table 3-2. *Azure products that are always free*

Product	Usage limit
Functions	One million requests per month
Machine Learning Service	Free; pay for Azure resources consumed
Machine Learning Studio	100 modules per experiment
Face API	30,000 transactions per month
Translator Text API	Two million characters
Azure DevOps	Five users (unlimited private Git repositories)
App Service	10 apps
Azure Kubernetes Service	Free
Microsoft IoT Hub	8,000 messages per day
Data Factory	Five activities low frequency
Service Fabric	Free

Azure General Services

With Azure, we have at our disposal many services:

Azure Functions
: Event-driven serverless compute service.

Cosmos DB
: Transparent scaling and replicating data service for global distribution across any number of Azure regions.

API Management
: Use API Management to publish APIs to external, partner, and employee developers, securely and at scale.

Blob Storage
: Massively scalable object storage for unstructured data.

Cognitive Services

Infuse your apps, websites, and bots with intelligent algorithms to see, hear, speak, understand, and interpret your users' needs through natural methods of communication.

Machine Learning Studio

A collaborative, drag-and-drop tool that you can use to build, test, and deploy predictive analytics solutions on your data. Machine Learning Studio publishes models as web services that can be easily consumed by custom apps or business intelligence (BI) tools such as Excel.

Azure Kubernetes Service

A fully managed Kubernetes container orchestration service.

Logic Apps

Integration solutions builder and workflow orchestrator.

IoT Hub

Connect, monitor, and manage billions of IoT assets.

Stream Analytics

Easily develop and run massively parallel real-time analytics on multiple IoT or non-IoT streams of data using simple SQL-like language.

SignalR Service

Allows bidirectional communication between server and client. Servers can now push content to connected clients instantly as it becomes available.

Content Delivery Network (CDN)

Lets you reduce load times, save bandwidth, and speed responsiveness.

Event Grid

A single service for managing routing of all events from any source to any destination.

Service Bus

A highly reliable cloud messaging service between applications and services, even when one or more is offline.

Event Hubs

A fully managed, real-time data ingestion service that's simple, trusted, and scalable. Stream millions of events per second from any source to build dynamic data pipelines and immediately respond to business challenges.

Data Lake
> Makes it easy for developers, data scientists, and analysts to store data of any size, shape, and speed, and do all types of processing and analytics across platforms and languages.

SQL Data Warehouse
> Fast, flexible, and secure cloud data warehouse for enterprises.

Data Factory
> Create, schedule, and manage your data integration at scale.

In this book, we mainly use Azure Functions, Cognitive Services, and Machine Learning Studio. We will need Blob Storage to store files as well as API Management and Cosmos DB for database management. Finally, we use Azure Kubernetes Service to prepare our own containers and deploy them to the cloud.

Azure Cognitive Services offers the following tools:

Vision
> Image-processing algorithms that are useful for interpreting what is in an image or video, recognizing written text and faces, and flagging content for moderation. Capabilities include:
>
> - Computer vision (images)
>   - Image classification
>   - Scene and activity recognition
>   - Celebrity and landmark recognition
>   - Optical character recognition (OCR)
>   - Handwriting recognition
>
> - Face (images)
>   - Face detection
>   - Person identification
>   - Emotion recognition
>   - Similar face recognition and grouping
>
> - Video indexer (videos)
>   - Face detection
>   - Object, scene, and activity detection
>   - Metadata, audio, and keyframe extraction and analysis

- Content moderator
  - Explicit or offensive content moderation for images and videos
  - Custom image and text lists to block or allow matching content
  - Tools for including feedback from human moderators
- Custom vision
  - Customizable image recognition

Knowledge

Map complex information and data for tasks such as intelligent recommendations and semantic search to build simple explanations of commonly requested information. Capabilities include:

- QnA Maker
  - QnA extraction from unstructured text
  - Knowledge base creation from collections of Q&As
  - Semantic matching for knowledge bases

Language

Process natural language, evaluate sentiment, and recognize what users want. Spell check and moderate text and contextual understanding. Capabilities include:

- Text analytics
  - Named entity recognition
  - Key phrase extraction
  - Text sentiment analysis
- Translator text
  - Automatic language detection
  - Automated text translation
  - Customizable translation
- Bing Spell Check
  - Web-scale, multilingual spell checking
  - Contextual spell checking
- Content moderator
  - Explicit or offensive content moderation for images and videos

- — Custom image and text lists to block or allow matching content
- — Tools for including feedback from human moderators
- Language understanding
  - — Contextual language understanding

Speech

Convert spoken audio into text, and text to speech. Use voice for verification, speaker recognition, and real-time translation. Capabilities include:

- Speech to text
  - — Automatic speech recognition and speech transcription (speech to text)
  - — Customizable speech recognition and speech transcription (speech to text)
  - — Customizable speech models for unique vocabularies or accents
- Speaker recognition
  - — Speaker identification
  - — Speaker verification
- Text to speech
  - — Automatic text to speech
  - — Customizable voice fonts for text to speech
- Speech translation
  - — Real-time translation
  - — Automated speech translation
  - — Customizable translation

Search

Add search APIs to your apps and harness the ability to comb billions of web pages, images, videos, and news feeds with a single API call. Use for autosuggestion, news search and trend identification, and to identify and classify entities. Capabilities include:

- Bing Web Search
- Bing Custom Search
- Bing Image Search
- Bing Local Business Search

- Bing Autosuggest
- Bing News Search
    - Trending topic identification

- Bing Video Search
    - Video topic and trend identification

- Bing Visual Search
    - Image identification and classification
    - Knowledge acquisition from images
    - Identification of similar images

- Bing Entity Search
    - Named entity recognition and classification
    - Knowledge acquisition for named entities

You can find more information about Cognitive Services at *https://azure.micro-soft.com/en-us/services/cognitive-services*.

## PART II

Adding Intelligence

## CHAPTER 4

Getting Started with Microsoft Azure Functions

In this chapter, we show you how to start creating serverless applications using Azure Functions, write basic functions using the Python programming language, and use Azure Blob to store and retrieve files and data.

Azure Functions

To begin working with Azure Functions, first you must understand the terminology that Azure uses for these services:

Functions

We call various functions in response to different events and return a result. Our functions are stateless in general but can interact with databases and other resources. With Azure Functions in the Consumption plan (pay-per-execution pricing model), functions by default should take no more than five minutes to execute. You can extend this to 10 minutes by changing the timeout property.

Function Apps

Several functions are grouped into Apps, which share a domain name for URI and other configurations. The Function App is the unit of scale. When the Function App is scaled out, additional resources are allocated to run multiple instances of the Azure Functions host. Conversely, as compute demand is reduced, the scale controller removes function host instances. The number of instances is eventually scaled down to zero when no functions are running within a Function App.

Functions Project

> This usually refers to the local folder in which all source code is stored for a particular Function App.

Resource group

> A collection of resources that share the same life cycle, permissions, and policies, so it is easier to assign directly to one or several Function Apps.

Triggers and bindings

> Triggers define how a function is invoked. A common trigger is an HTTP/S call for a REST API interaction, but you can invoke functions in several different ways. For example, a function can be invoked automatically when a file is created in the storage area or when data changes in a database. You can optionally add input and output bindings to the configuration of a function, describing data from related services that should be available for the function to process.

Let's now create a Function App via the Azure Portal. We'll show you how to install all the prerequisites for local development and create a Functions Project on your local computer, add a function to it that is triggered by an HTTP request event, launch it locally to test the function, and deploy it to the Function App to test it again online. We'll also look at how to use Visual Studio Code to create new Function Projects and to create, run, and debug new functions.

Creating a Function App by Using Azure Portal

The first thing you need to do is create an Azure account (*https://azure.micro soft.com/es-es/free/serverless/*).

> Please remember that this URL and other URLs in this book may change in the future.

On the Azure Portal dashboard (see Figure 4-1), in the panel on the left side, click "Create a resource." Then, in the list of resources that opens, select Function Apps.

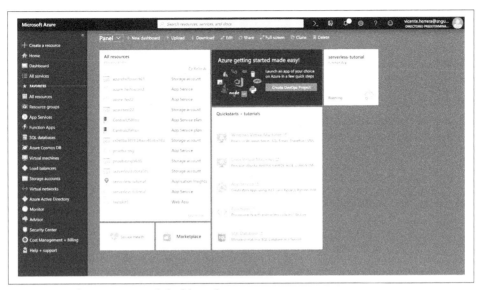

Figure 4-1. The Azure Portal dashboard

You'll be presented with several options that you can customize:

App name
This name will also be used for the URL of the resources you create in the Function App.

Subscription
The payment account that will be used.

Resource group
A name to group several Azure services that you want to manage together. Select "Create new."

 Python Functions-as-a-Service (FaaS) is in a preview stage as of this writing. This means that we can use it and it is well documented, but some features might not be optimized or fully available. Microsoft rarely leaves new services in a preview state for long; this is a way to give users an advance look at the technology.

Now you need to choose some specific options (see Figure 4-2):

OS
Choose Linux.

Publish
Select Code.

Runtime Stack

Set this to Python.

Storage

Where code will be stored in Azure. Select "Create new."

Application Insights

Activate this to collect monitoring data and receive recommendations about usage and optimization of your Function App.

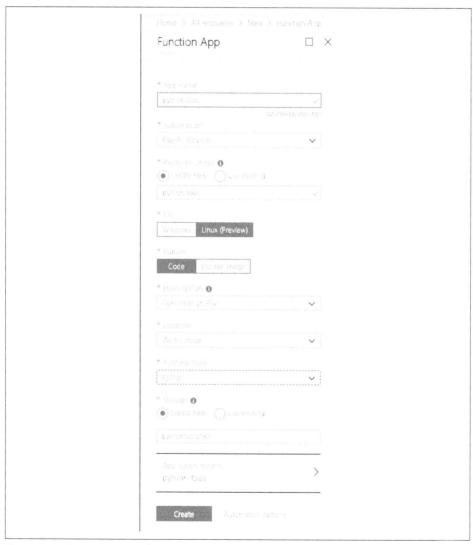

Figure 4-2. Setting options for a Function App

Click Create. It takes several minutes for the creation process to finish, and a notification will inform you when the process is done. When you see it, your Function App is ready! You can click the notification message, which is a quick link that will appear on the dashboard, as shown in Figure 4-3; or, in the menu on the left, select "All resources" and then search for your Function App to start working on it.

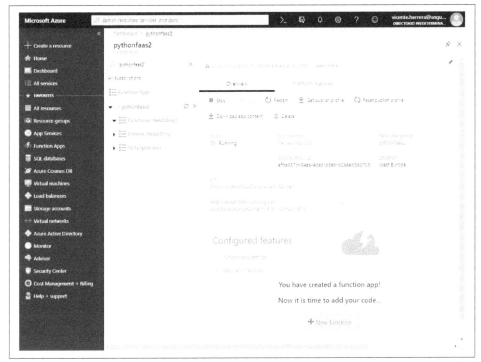

Figure 4-3. The Azure dashboard showing the notification that your Function App is ready

On the Function App web page, you can start, stop, or restart the app and change many options; for example, you can define a custom domain, change the authentication/authorization settings and the CORS security definition, and configure monitoring and metrics.

At the bottom of the page, click "New function." You'll be asked if you want to program it using "VS Code" or "Any editor + Core Tools," as illustrated in Figure 4-4. Whichever you choose, you'll be presented with a brief tutorial on how to use those tools to program functions, but we'll also give you a more detailed explanation later in this chapter.

If you had selected a different programming language—for example, JavaScript—you would have a third option that allowed you to program new functions within the Portal using a basic online code editor. Using the Portal editor is a good exercise if you want to test simple things within your functions, but you eventually will need a local development environment for full-fledged function creation.

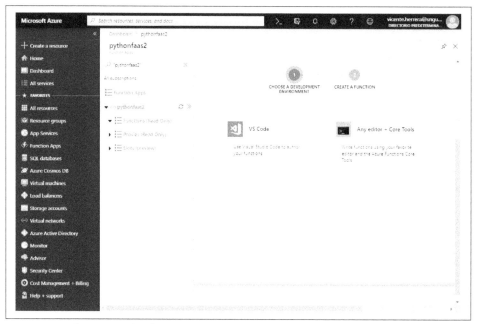

Figure 4-4. Choosing a development environment

Local Development Environment

Now you need to prepare your local environment to code functions. First, you need to install all the prerequisites. All software referenced in the subsections that follow is open source and available for any operating system.

.NET Core v2.x

Azure Functions run on the .NET runtime in Azure or on your computer. You must install it even if you're not going to use a .NET language.

.NET Core is the new implementation of the .NET platform as an open source project under the .NET Foundation. It is compatible with the latest version of .NET Framework that was available only on Windows, but in the future the framework will be discontinued and all further development will rely on .NET Core.

.NET Core differs on .NET Framework in that it has a modular architecture in which you can install and upgrade individual components using NuGet, whereas .NET Framework requires a full update of the framework to fix things or deploy new features. That makes development in .NET Core more agile.

You can download .NET Core v2.x from the Microsoft website (*https://dotnet.micro soft.com/download*).

Package manager

To install Azure Functions Core Tools later, you will need a package manager to handle the installation and future updates:

- For Linux, you can use the existing package manager of your distribution.
- For macOS, use Homebrew (*https://brew.sh*).
- For Windows, one of the alternatives is Chocolatey (*https://chocolatey.org/*).

You also can use Node.js to install Core Tools on Windows.

Node.js

Node.js is not essential for programming in Python, but it is necessary to program functions in JavaScript or to install Azure Core Tools on Windows without using Chocolatey.

When using it with Functions, you might encounter an error informing you to use the latest version, like 10.6, when you already have a stable one like 11.x. To prevent that, we recommend that you install the Node Version Manager tool (nvm) (*https://github.com/creationix/nvm*).

Then, use it to switch to Node.js version 10.6.0 by using the following command:

```
nvm install 10.6.0
```

You might need to reinstall globally installed Node Package Manager (npm) packages after the switch. You can check whether the correct version is running by using this command:

```
node -v
```

Azure Functions Core Tools 2

Azure Functions Core Tools is a command-line tool that you can use to create new Functions Projects, add code for new Functions to them, execute them on your local machine, deploy them online, and much more.

We will use version 2.x, which enables the usage of Python. After all the prerequisites are satisfied, it's easy to install.

On Linux Ubuntu 18.04, use these commands:

```
wget -q https://packages.microsoft.com/config/ubuntu/18.04/
    packages-microsoft-prod.deb
sudo dpkg -i packages-microsoft-prod.deb
sudo apt-get update
sudo apt-get install azure-functions-core-tools
```

For other Linux distributions, use these instructions (*http://bit.ly/2UAMTur*).

You can also install it on macOS, using Homebrew:

```
brew tap azure/functions
brew install azure-functions-core-tools
```

on Windows, using Chocolatey on an administration command line:

```
choco install azure-functions-core-tools
```

or using npm:

```
npm i -g azure-functions-core-tools --unsafe-perm true
```

Python 3.6 on Linux Ubuntu 18

Python 3.6 is already installed in Linux Ubuntu 18, but there are a couple of things you still need to take into consideration. First, instead of calling python from the command line, you should use python3. And you need to install the virtual environment tool for Python by using the following command:

```
apt-get install python3-env
```

Python 3.6 on Windows

You need the Python SDK to use it as a programming language. As of this writing, Azure Functions requires Python to be version 3.6, specifically. If you are new to Python, you should know that Python 2.x and Python 3.x usually coexist on many machines, as many packages support 2.x but might not be totally compatible with 3.x.

As just mentioned, Azure Functions requires Python 3.6, but the latest version of Python is 3.7, so installing the latest version is not suggested. If you've accidentally upgraded, just download the 3.6 installer (*https://www.python.org/downloads/*). Remember on installation to select the option to "Add Python 3.6 to PATH," as shown in Figure 4-5.

By default, the installation directory will be:

```
c:\users\<username>\AppData\Local\Programs\Python\Python36
```

But you can change it to something shorter for all users, like this, by selecting "Customize installation":

```
C:\python\python36
```

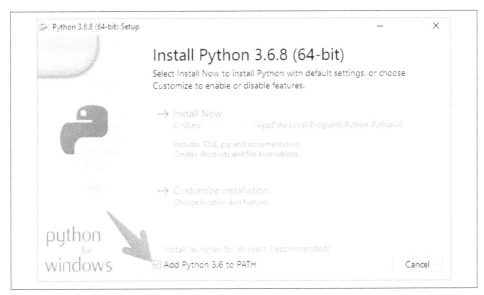

Figure 4-5. Installing Python 3.6

Python 3.6 on macOS

Python 2.x is already installed on macOS, and the operating system uses it for some things, so you don't want to tamper with that version. You can identify which version of Python is running by using the following at the command line:

```
python -V
```

Homebrew always installs the latest version of a program by default, but you can instruct it to use an older one by specifying the hash of its repository URL. Here's how to do that for Python 3.6.7:

```
brew unlink python
brew install https://raw.githubusercontent.com/Homebrew/homebrew-core/
    f2a764ef944b1080be64bd88dca9a1d80130c558/Formula/python.rb
```

You might encounter an error linking to the */user/local/Frameworks* folder. If this happens, you must create that directory (and reinstall it again):

```
sudo mkdir /usr/local/Frameworks
sudo chown $(whoami):admin /usr/local/Frameworks
```

When you have several versions of Python installed with Homebrew, you can see a list of them using the following:

```
brew info python
```

You can switch to a different version with:

```
brew switch python 3.6.7
```

Take into consideration that packages installed using the `pip` tool for Python might need to be reinstalled when switching versions.

An alternative for this that might or might not work for you is to use the `pyenv` tool to manage Python versions, which you can install as follows:

```
xcode-select --install
brew update
brew install pyenv
```

Then you can install and change Python versions by using these commands:

```
pyenv install 3.6.7
pyenv global 3.6.7
```

If you get a "zlib not available" error on macOS Mojave, specify the header libraries by using this command:

```
sudo xcode-select -s /Library/Developer/CommandLineTools
```

Or, specify the actual location:

```
CFLAGS="-I$(xcrun --show-sdk-path)/usr/include" pyenv install -v 3.6.7
```

Or, if you installed `zlib` with Homebrew, set `CPPFLAGS` by doing the following:

```
CPPFLAGS="-I$(brew --prefix zlib)/include" pyenv install -v 3.6.7
```

You might experience some slight differences on Linux systems.

 Git (*https://git-scm.com/download*) is the most popular version control system, and it might already be installed on your computer. It is not mandatory to use it, but any time you create a Functions Project, Core Tools will also initialize a new Git repository in it.

Creating a Functions Project Using Core Tools

To create a new Functions Project, you should use a *Python virtual environment*. This is a hidden folder in which Python stores copies of all dependencies (including the Python executable version) alongside necessary Python packages. This means that any time you execute the project, on any machine, it will run under exactly the right conditions and with the right dependencies already available.

The commands that follow create a directory, change into it, create a Python virtual environment, activate it, get out of the directory, and use the Core Tools `func` command-line tool to initialize the Functions Project. The order is important because `func` requires the Python virtual environment to be created and active before creating the Functions Project.

On macOS and Linux, using a Bash shell, the commands are as follows:

```
mkdir myproject
cd myproject
python -m venv .env
source ./.env/bin/activate
cd ..
func init myproject
```

You can find different *activate* scripts in the *.env/bin* directory for different shells, like fish.

Creating the project on Windows with *cmd.exe* is similar:

```
mkdir myproject
cd myproject
python -m venv .env
.\.env\bin\activate.bat
cd ..
func init myproject
```

You'll be asked what runtime you want to use; choose Python. After that, several files will be generated in your directory.

You should also enter that directory and install or update `pip` (to install other packages), `ptvsd` (to debug Python files), and `pylint` (a linter to check for code mistakes). You might already have those installed in your global Python, but it might be necessary to install them again in your recently activated Python virtual environment:

```
cd myproject
python -m pip install --upgrade pip
python -m pip install --upgrade ptvsd
python -m pip install --upgrade pylint
```

Creating new functions using Core Tools

You have activated a Python virtual environment and have an empty Functions Project. Let's add a new function using Core Tools:

```
func new
```

You'll be asked to select a template from a list. The choices include general triggers:

- An HTTP trigger to trigger the execution of your code by using an HTTP request
- An Azure Blob Storage trigger to process storage blobs when they are added to containers
- An Azure Cosmos DB trigger to process Cosmos DB documents when they are added or updated in collections in a NoSQL database

and event- and queue-related triggers:

- An Azure Event Grid trigger to respond to events delivered to a subscription in Azure Event Grid
- An Azure Event Hub trigger to respond to events delivered to an Azure Event Hub
- An Azure Queue Storage trigger to respond to messages as they arrive in an Azure Storage queue
- An Azure Service Bus Queue trigger to connect to other Azure or on-premises service message queues
- An Azure Service Bus Topic trigger to connect to other Azure services or on-premises services by subscribing to topics
- A Timer trigger to execute a function on a predefined schedule

If you don't understand much of the previous list, don't worry. The most important item is the HTTP trigger; the rest you can learn about later when you use the related Azure services.

Choose "HTTP trigger." This means that your new function will activate when the app receives an HTTP call (like the one a browser makes when it requests a web page from a server). This is what is used in a REST API, whereas other kinds of *clients* connect to our API endpoints using HTTP requests.

We will need to provide a name for the function—in this case we will call it, very simply, HttpTrigger—and a new directory will be created in the project with that name. Inside of it, there will be three files:

function.json
    Configuration file for our function

Sample.dat
    Sample data to test the function

__init__.py
    The main file with the code that our function runs

Let's take a look at each of these, starting with the most important one (the one that has the code for the function), *__init__.py*:

```
import logging
import azure.functions as func
def main(req: func.HttpRequest) -> func.HttpResponse:
    logging.info('Python HTTP trigger function processed a request.')
    name = req.params.get('name')
    if not name:
        try:
```

```
        req_body = req.get_json()
    except ValueError:
        pass
    else:
        name = req_body.get('name')
if name:
    return func.HttpResponse(f"Hello {name}!")
else:
    return func.HttpResponse(
        "Please pass a name in the query string or in the request body",
        status_code=400
    )
```

In this case, Core Tools generated an example function called main based on an example template for an HTTP request function. It takes a parameter, req, that is of type func.HttpRequest and returns a parameter also of type func.HttpResponse.

In the req.params object you will find all of the HTTP parameters passed in the URL, and you should expect a name parameter to be present, which you can read from req.params.name. You can use this to build a greeting message.

Let's take a closer look at this function. It's very simple. When you visit the URL that triggers the execution of the function, either you'll see a message indicating that a name should be provided or, if you passed the name using a URL parameter, a friendly "Hello <name>" will be shown. Now let's look in more detail at the execution of this function.

What will be returned to the user will be in the form of an HttpResponse, which has a body of text and, optionally, a status code (if not supplied, the status 200 OK will be used). These codes are standard for many kinds of HTTP status responses and are meant to make it easy to detect an error when it happens, no matter what the text message is, or an unchanged resource that can be cached. They're also important because codes of the 4xx (request can't be fulfilled) and 5xx (errors) type are not billed by Azure. Any time you test for an error or a resource not found, you should return one of those codes.

Starting the Function App locally using Core Tools

To test your function, you need to start the Function App locally using Core Tools via this command:

```
func host start
```

Core Tools starts a local instance of the Azure Functions runtime, with all functions waiting for events to arrive and, at the end of the log, information about how they can be triggered:

```
Now listening on: http://0.0.0.0:7071
Application started. Press Ctrl+C to shut down.
```

```
Http Functions:
        HttpTrigger: [GET,POST] http://localhost:7071/api/HttpTrigger
[13/01/2019 22:20:09] Host lock lease acquired by instance ID
    '000000000000000000000000005E6E4E8'.
```

This says the Function App is running, it's listening at the URL *http://localhost:7071/api/HttpTrigger*, and it's listening to the verbs GET and POST. If you try to visit that URL, a message that you already have seen in your code appears in the browser:

```
Please pass a name in the query string or in the request body
```

You must pass a name parameter, which you can do by using a URL like this:

```
http://localhost:7071/api/HttpTrigger?name=Vicente
```

Here's what you get:

```
Hello Vicente!
```

So, the function waits for an HTTP request event, like the one a browser makes when visiting a web page, then runs with the parameters provided, and then returns some output. This means that you can use your browser for testing.

Function settings files

Let's take a look at the rest of the files inside the function folder. *Sample.dat* is very small and not so important; it has only an example parameter set to automate testing the function:

```
{
    "name": "Azure"
}
```

Azure generates this test automatically based on your code.

But *function.json* is very important, having several configuration parameters:

```
{
  "scriptFile": "__init__.py",
  "bindings": [
    {
      "authLevel": "anonymous",
      "type": "httpTrigger",
      "direction": "in",
      "name": "req",
      "methods": [
        "get",
        "post"
      ]
    },
    {
      "type": "http",
      "direction": "out",
      "name": "$return"
```

```
    }
  ]
}
```

The methods section is an array of the different HTTP verbs this function accepts, so you can program several different functions that process the same URL depending on the method used for the query. Because the directory name is the default URL for the function, to do so you need to add a parameter to *function.json* to explicitly change that URL, using the route key.

If you were to create a function that instead of receiving a name value as a parameter read it from the URL, the *function.json* file would be as follows:

```
{
  "scriptFile": "__init__.py",
  "bindings": [
    {
      "authLevel": "anonymous",
      "type": "httpTrigger",
      "direction": "in",
      "name": "req",
      "route": "hello/{name}",
      "methods": [
        "get"
      ]
    },
    {
      "type": "http",
      "direction": "out",
      "name": "$return"
    }
  ]
}
```

If you then changed your function's code so that instead of using this:

```
name = req.params.get('name')
```

it used this:

```
name = req.route_params.get('name')
```

you could execute the function just by using a URL of the form:

```
http://localhost:7071/api/hello/vicente
```

Local settings and production settings

Another file that you will find in the root directory of your project is *local.set-tings.json*. This file stores settings that should be taken into consideration in your application only if it is executed from your local environment, not when deployed to Azure. You usually define here connection strings to databases and other key–value

pairs of "secrets." All those values will be accessible from your code in the pro
cess.env variable.

Here are the contents of *local.settings.json*:

```
{
  "IsEncrypted": false,
  "Values": {
    "FUNCTIONS_WORKER_RUNTIME": "python",
    "AzureWebJobsStorage": ""
  }
}
```

This file is ignored by default in the Git repository, so you can store sensitive data in
it without worrying if the repository is read later. When deploying your Functions
Project to Azure, you should visit your Function App dashboard and set the values
for the settings used, but using the data that they should have for the production
environment. Click the "Application settings" link and then scroll to the section also
named "Application settings" to set their production values, as demonstrated in
Figure 4-6.

Figure 4-6. Adjusting settings in the Function App dashboard

Deployment using Core Tools

When you want to deploy your Functions Project code to your already created Function App on the Azure Portal, you can use the command line. If you have your virtual environment active, from the project's root directory, just type the following:

```
func azure functionapp publish <app_name> --build-native-deps
```

The first time you run it, it should ask you to ensure you have the Azure CLI installed and to log in to Azure Portal to proceed. From that moment on, it will reuse your credentials and you won't be asked again. Then, a Docker image will be provisioned to compile the Python project and dependencies to native Linux binaries for execution on the Azure platform, and everything will be packed and uploaded to your Function App. At the end, a list of your functions with a URL for each one will be provided, as shown here:

```
Getting site publishing info...
pip download -r C:\Users\vicen\code\pytest\requirements.txt
   --dest C:\Users\vicen\AppData\Local\Temp\azureworkerm0zb5f03
pip download --no-deps --only-binary :all: --platform manylinux1_x86_64
   --python-version 36 --implementation cp --abi cp36m
   --dest C:\Users\vicen\AppData\Local\Temp\azureworkerqdfgfduv
   azure_functions==1.0.0b3 pip download --no-deps --only-binary
   :all: --platform manylinux1_x86_64 --python-version 36 --implementation cp
   --abi cp36m --dest C:\Users\vicen\AppData\Local\Temp\azureworkerqdfgfduv
   azure_functions_worker==1.0.0b3
pip download --no-deps --only-binary :all: --platform manylinux1_x86_64
   --python-version 36 --implementation cp --abi cp36m
   --dest C:\Users\vicen\AppData\Local\Temp\azureworkerqdfgfduv grpcio==1.14.2
pip download --no-deps --only-binary :all: --platform manylinux1_x86_64
   --python-version 36 --implementation cp --abi cp36m
   --dest C:\Users\vicen\AppData\Local\Temp\azureworkerqdfgfduv grpcio_tools==1.14.2
pip download --no-deps --only-binary :all: --platform manylinux1_x86_64
   --python-version 36 --implementation cp --abi cp36m
   --dest C:\Users\vicen\AppData\Local\Temp\azureworkerqdfgfduv protobuf==3.7.0
pip download --no-deps --only-binary :all: --platform manylinux1_x86_64
   --python-version 36 --implementation cp --abi cp36m
   --dest C:\Users\vicen\AppData\Local\Temp\azureworkerqdfgfduv setuptools==40.8.0
pip download --no-deps --only-binary :all: --platform manylinux1_x86_64
   --python-version 36 --implementation cp --abi cp36m
   --dest C:\Users\vicen\AppData\Local\Temp\azureworkerqdfgfduv six==1.12.0

Preparing archive...
Uploading 55.71 MB [###############################################]
Upload completed successfully.
Deployment completed successfully.
Syncing triggers...
Functions in python-serverless:
      HttpTrigger - [httpTrigger]
    Invoke url: https://python-serverless.azurewebsites.net/api/
    httptrigger?code=B7HJdw62THNLL9lVWWm6jaf3GSrzGRHRafvYBUTgBrqp234J3bkzZA-=
```

The URL that triggers your function is presented here as the following:

```
https://python-serverless.azurewebsites.net/api/
    httptrigger?code=B7HJdw62THNLL9lVWWm6jaf3GSrzGRHRafvYBUTgBrqp234J3bkzZA-=
```

That includes the Function App master key (which changes upon every execution) after `code=`, but if the access level of your function is `anonymous`, you are not required to send it in your call. Instead you can just use this:

```
https://python-serverless.azurewebsites.net/api/httptrigger
```

 We explain more about access levels in Chapter 7.

So, visiting that last URL with a browser, you should see again the same message for the missing parameter:

```
Please pass a name in the query string or in the request body
```

And when you add the `name` parameter to it:

```
https://python-serverless.azurewebsites.net/api/httptrigger?name=Vicente
```

you will see again:

```
Hello Vicente!
```

Congratulations! You have created your first Function App using the Azure Portal, created a Functions Project on your local computer, added a function to it that is triggered by an HTTP request event, and deployed it to the Function App. And it all works!

Using Visual Studio Code

To edit the code of our functions, we use Microsoft's open source code editor available for all operating systems, Visual Studio Code. Visual Studio Code is well regarded by many programmers, especially in the JavaScript community. You will see that it has several specific extensions to help with Azure Functions. Before we get underway, though, we need to set it up to program Python Functions Projects.

Because Python support in Functions is still recent and in preview, some of the options for that programming language in Visual Studio Code are not available to use, like deployment (you should continue to use the command-line tool `func`). But we are confident that they will be added very soon, given that new versions of all these components are released frequently.

Here's the web page from which you can download and install Visual Studio Code (*https://code.visualstudio.com/*).

To get started, in the vertical menu bar on the left (see Figure 4-7), click the icon for extensions (▣) and then search for these extensions:

Azure Tools extension collection (http://bit.ly/2P8Tmqd)
This is a collection of several extensions for working with Azure services like Functions, Cosmos DB, App Service, and Storage.

Python extension for Visual Studio Code (http://bit.ly/2G7LdOL)
This allows you to debug Python code in a Functions Project.

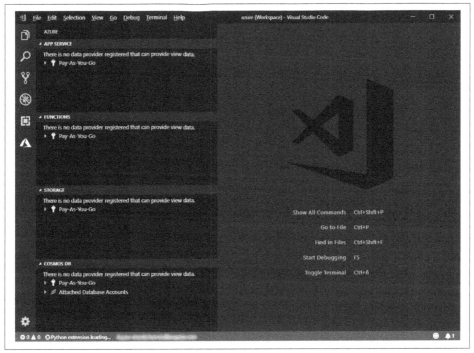

Figure 4-7. Getting started with Visual Studio Code

Again, in the menu bar on the left, click the Azure icon (🔺) to change to the Azure view, and then click "Sign in to Azure." A browser session opens in which you can authenticate on the Azure Portal and link the Azure extensions to use your Azure account, as shown in Figure 4-8.

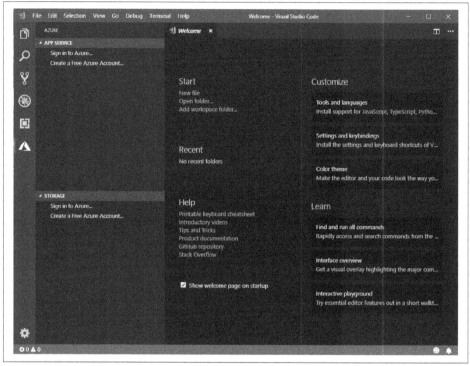

Figure 4-8. Authenticating on the Azure Portal

To create a project more quickly and easily than using the command-line Core tools, hover your pointer over the Functions group and click the "Create new project" icon (![icon]). You can also create a new function from within a project by using the "New function" icon (![icon]) and deploy a Functions Project to an already created Function App on Azure by using the deploy button (![icon]).

By right-clicking the subscription name, you can do the following:

- Open a browser to the Azure Portal.
- Create a Function App in Azure without opening the Portal. This currently works only for the Windows runtime. To select a Linux runtime to be able to program in Python, you will need to create it in the Azure Portal, as described.

When you click on the subscription name, a list of all your Function Apps hosted in Azure shows. Right-click any of them and you have several options:

- Open the app in the Portal.
- Start, stop, or restart the app.

- Delete the Function App.
- Deploy the Function App (still doesn't work for Python Functions Projects).
- Configure the deployment source.
- Start or stop streaming online logs for the app.

To access the debug window, click the debugger icon (). There, you can click the small play icon (the right-facing green triangle shown in Figure 4-9) to start debugging your app (or press the F5 key without having to switch to the debug sidebar first).

Figure 4-9. The Debug window

You can add your existing Functions Project to the workspace, and it will be recognized by Visual Studio Code, as depicted in Figure 4-10. This allows you to add some helpful configuration.

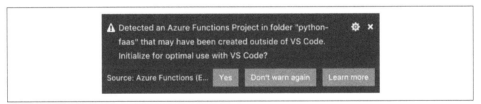

Figure 4-10. Functions Project detection

Switch from custom shells to Bash in Visual Studio Code

The Visual Studio Code "debug run" command for Function Apps is written *for Bash on non-Windows operating systems*; it is not compatible with other shells like fish. If the default shell on your system is not Bash, you should change to whichever shell Visual Studio Code should use. To do that, go to the settings, search for "shell," and then change it by clicking Terminal → Integrated → Shell:

- From: */usr/local/bin/fish* (or whatever value you have different from */bin/bash*)
- To: */bin/bash*

Debugging Python by Using Visual Studio Code

Let's see how debugging works in Visual Studio Code. Add your Functions Project to the workspace, open your function's *__init__.py* file, and then double-click to the left of line 9 in the code. A red dot appears, indicating that you just added a breakpoint.

Press F5 to run your code, and watch the execution log in the integrated terminal. If you are asked which Python to use, as illustrated in Figure 4-11, choose the one residing in your *.env* folder.

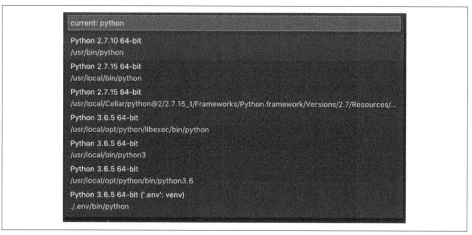

Figure 4-11. Selecting a Python version (choose the one that's in your .env folder)

Now, if you visit the URL *http://localhost:7071/api/HttpTrigger?name=Vicente* with your browser or trigger the endpoint with any sort of API client, Visual Studio Code will gain focus, appearing in front of other windows on your system; execution of the Function App will stop at the first line with a breakpoint in your code, and that file will be shown in the editor.

You might run into some problems, though. Let's run through and try to solve them.

Problem: Configured debug type 'python' is not supported

When you start debugging, you might encounter the error message depicted in Figure 4-12.

Figure 4-12. Error message: debug type not supported

To solve this problem, simply install the Python extension for Visual Studio Code (*http://bit.ly/2G7LdOL*).

Problem: Forbidden execution of scripts (Windows)

When you start debugging in Windows, you might encounter the problem depicted in Figure 4-13.

```
PROBLEMS   OUTPUT   TERMINAL   ...                    1: Task - runFunctionsH ▾   ✚  ⊟  🗑  ∧  ✖

> Executing task in folder python-faas: .env\Scripts\activate ; func extensions install ;
pip install -r requirements.txt ; func host start <

.env\Scripts\activate : No se puede cargar el archivo
C:\Users\vicen\Documents\_azure\python-faas\.env\Scripts\Activate.ps1 porque la
ejecución de scripts está deshabilitada en este sistema. Para obtener más información,
consulta el tema about_Execution_Policies en
https://go.microsoft.com/fwlink/?LinkID=135170.
En línea: 1 Carácter: 1
+ .env\Scripts\activate ; func extensions install ; pip install -r requ ...
+ ~~~~~~~~~~~~~~~~~~~~~~
    + CategoryInfo          : SecurityError: (:) [], PSSecurityException
    + FullyQualifiedErrorId : UnauthorizedAccess
```

Figure 4-13. Debugging in Windows

To solve this problem, you need to activate execution of scripts. Start PowerShell as an administrator and then run the following command:

```
Set-ExecutionPolicy Unrestricted
```

Problem: Failed to attach, no module named ptvsd

When you try to start the debugger on any operating system, a message like that shown in Figure 4-14 might appear.

```
                          ✖  Failed to attach (connect ECONNREFUSED 127.0.0.1:9091)

                                          Open launch.json        Cancel
```

Figure 4-14. Error message when starting the debugger

Also, in the Visual Studio Code terminal window, the log will show a message similar to that shown in Figure 4-15.

```
[06/01/2019 10:50:33] C:\Python\Python36\python.exe: No module named ptvsd
[06/01/2019 10:50:33] Language Worker Process exited.
[06/01/2019 10:50:33] python exited with code 1
```

Figure 4-15. Error in the Visual Studio Code terminal window

To solve this problem, first install `ptvsd` globally, as shown here:

```
pip install ptvsd
```

Then activate your virtual environment and also install it locally:

```
python -m pip install --upgrade ptvsd
```

Azure Blob Storage

You now know a little about programming functions, but to build a more complex application, you need to interface with data storage systems. With this in mind, Azure offers the Blob service.

A *blob*, or *binary large object*, is a piece of unstructured data such as text or binary data. After it is stored, it has a unique HTTP/S system that you can use with private access or open it to share with anyone. All blobs are stored in *blob containers* that work in a similar way to folders on your computer.

If you are going to write or read data in text files from your functions or feed data to train your machine learning modules, you are going to use blobs. Azure Blob is also the main tool for big data analysis, and you can use it to store static assets for websites, like HTML, CSS, frontend JavaScript, and image files.

Azure Blob is very easy to integrate with your functions, and it has many useful features:

- Scaling (scale up or down as your needs change, and pay only for what you use)
- Different tiers for frequently accessed (hot tier), infrequently accessed (cold tier), and rarely accessed (archive storage tier) data
- Georedundancy, which means that the service runs in several geographical locations as a redundancy in case the primary system fails for any reason
- Block, page, and append types of blobs, so you can optimize their configuration for the kind of data processing that you will do

You might not know it, but you are already working with blobs. Remember when you created your Function App, and you were asked whether you wanted to create a new object storage or use an existing one? The one that you created is in fact a blob storage. You will often find that *data storage* and *blob* are synonymous in the Azure ecosystem.

Creating a Storage Account

Go to the Azure Portal and click All Resources. If you followed the steps in the previous section to create a Function App, you will see several elements there. One of these should be of type "storage account," accompanied by this icon: . It contains the source code for the execution of the Function App. With some exceptions, you could reuse it for other purposes. For example, if you want to host static website files, you must create a new storage account and you can't use it at the same time for the code of a Function App.

Let's create a new account. In the menu on the left, click "Create a resource" and then choose Storage Account.

For a new account, you are asked to enter the following information:

- Project details:

  Subscription
  Choose your payment account.

  Resource group
  Create or reuse a group to manage together related Azure services used for the same project.

- Instance details:

  Storage account name
  Choose a valid name; this will be part of the unique URL of the blobs.

  Location
  Choose the closest to you.

  Performance
  Choose Standard; Premium will have better performance and provide a service-level agreement (SLA), but it will cost you.

  Account kind
  Choose StorageV2 for general-purpose uses.

  Replication
  Choose "Read-access geo-redundant storage (RA-GRS)" to have replication for read access across several locations. This will speed read access to blobs when not close to the original location.

  Access tier
  Choose Hot to store information that will be accessed frequently.

- Advanced:

  Security
  Secure transfer required: Enabled (to force using HTTPS and SSL).

  Virtual networks
  Allow access from: All networks.

  Data lake storage Gen2 (Preview) Hierarchical namespace: Disable.

- Tags:

  Name:Value
    Choose some key–value pairs if you want your storage accounts so that it is easier to find them when you have lots.

On the "Review + create" tab, click the Create button, and then wait for a notification that the storage account has been created.

Transferring Blobs

You can visit your new storage account in the "All resources" section of the Azure Portal. There, you can see a number of settings at your disposal for the storage account. First, let's use the Blob service to store files. Click the Blobs link; an empty list of blob containers appears. Click the icon to create a new one. When naming containers, you can use only lowercase letters and dashes, the initial character must be a letter or a number, and you can't use two dashes in a row. Also, the length of the name must be between 3 and 63 characters. You can also specify public read access for each blob in the new container, or the list of all the containers' blobs. Let's keep it private in this case.

Click within your new container; a new empty list of files and folders appears. You can now click Upload to send files to the container, and if you view the Advanced section, you can even put them in a separate folder in the container, as shown in Figure 4-16.

Then, when you click the uploaded file, you see a settings page for that item, and there is also a Download button so that you can get a copy to your current computer.

This is an interesting way of working with files, but it's not the most practical. Luckily, Microsoft offers a free program (*https://azure.microsoft.com/en-us/features/storage-explorer/*) called Azure Storage Explorer that is available for Windows, Linux, and macOS and makes viewing and managing blobs more practical.

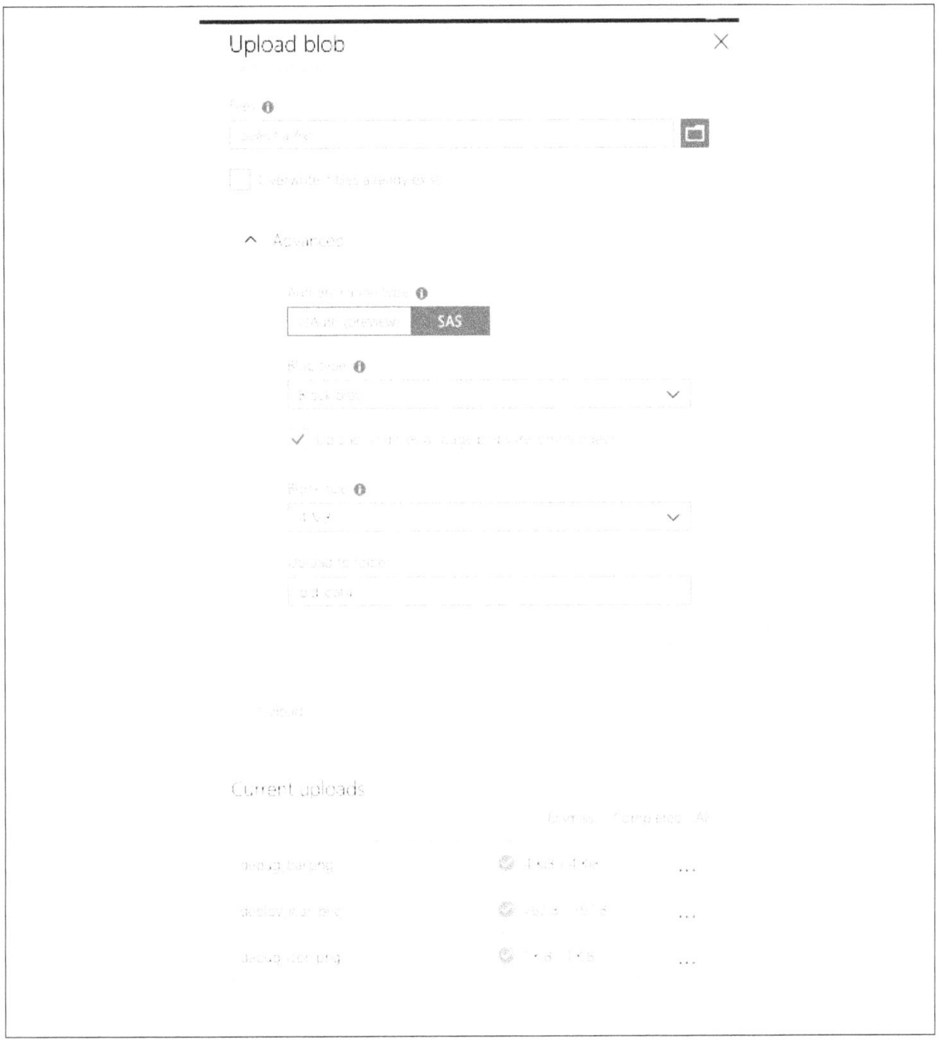

Figure 4-16. Transferring blobs in Azure Portal

After you install Storage Explorer, you can sign in to your Azure account, and it will show you a list of all the resources and activated services that you have created using the Azure Portal (see Figure 4-17). Among them, you will find the Storage Accounts section. If you expand any of the storage accounts, then expand Blob Containers, and then click one of the blob containers, you will see a list of all the files and folders inside. Storage Explorer makes it easy to upload or download files and folders, or to create or delete new blob containers and folders.

Figure 4-17. Azure Storage Explorer

There are many advanced settings that you can manage using Storage Explorer, but for now you've done everything necessary to proceed. You have your storage account with a blob container where you can upload or download files and folders that you can process with your functions.

Summary and Look Ahead

In this chapter, we explored setting up your Azure programming environment and preparing your machine, whether it's Windows, Linux, or macOS, and how to begin building your serverless systems.

In Chapter 5, we begin implementing machine learning models as we explore Azure's extensive collection of ready-made tools.

Using Machine Learning and Deep Learning Models

In this chapter, we examine the use of machine learning models in the cloud. First, we talk about prebuilt and pretrained machine learning services on Azure that we can deploy in a serverless environment. You need no machine learning knowledge to do this.

Then, we explore general machine learning tools such as Jupyter Notebook as well as widely used libraries such as Microsoft Cognitive Toolkit, ML.NET, TensorFlow, scikit-learn, and Keras. This chapter includes brief descriptions of these elements, using terminology that can be difficult to grasp for those without prior knowledge of machine learning.

Last but not least, we talk specifically about cloud machine learning and deep learning services available from Microsoft and show you how to use them in your applications. In this section, you will gain insight into tools like Machine Learning Studio as well as more powerful and sophisticated offerings like Azure Machine Learning Service.

Azure Cognitive Services

The Azure Portal offers several resources that are grouped in what is known as Cognitive Services, which enable you to add machine learning algorithms to your apps, web pages, and bots that in turn empower users to see, hear, speak, understand, and interpret user needs through natural methods of communication. These resources include prebuilt machine learning and deep learning modules that help with the following:

- Recognizing faces
- Sentiment analysis
- Content moderation
- Language understanding (LUIS)
- Text analytics
- Text to speech
- Voice recognition
- Personalized recommendations

Learning to use the resources in Cognitive Services is surprisingly simple. In this section you'll learn how to register and use Cognitive Services, and we'll develop this example by adding Cognitive Services to a complete Function App.

Setting Up and Using a Service in Cognitive Services

Let's begin with an example using the Cognitive Services Translator Text service. In this example, you will build an app that takes text in English as an input and outputs it in Spanish. The steps to achieve this will be similar to setting up other services in Cognitive Services. Microsoft Translator is a cloud-based machine translation service. The core service is the Translator Text API, a REST API URL to which we will make calls.

To develop the translation app you will need the service keys for the new service, which must be included in each call to the Translator Text API in order to authenticate your calls.

To obtain a key in the Azure Portal, select "Create a resource," search for and select Translator Text, and then click Create. You will be asked for the following information:

Name
    Provide a name.

Subscription
    Select your payment account.

Pricing tier
    Select F0 for a free trial, S1 for a pay-as-you-go model, or one of the other volume pricing offerings that will be presented to you.

Resource group
    Select "Create new."

Resource group location

Choose the one nearest to you.

After a few moments, a message will appear indicating that the new service has been created. Click the notification to go to the new resource or search for it in the "All resources" section. When you reach the translation resource page, you will find a link to the keys in the main window of the service. Two keys are shown; you can use either of them.

Let's write some local Python code to test the connectivity to the service. First, you need to install the Python libraries uuid (used to generate a universal unique identifier for your app) and requests (to send and manage the REST API requests):

```
pip install requests uuid
```

Next, write a file called *translate.py* with this content, into which you can paste one of your own subscription keys:

```
# -*- coding: utf-8 -*-
import os, requests, uuid, json
subscriptionKey = 'paste_your_key_here'
base_url = 'https://api.cognitive.microsofttranslator.com'
path = '/translate?api-version=3.0'
params = '&to=es' # We leave source language to be autodetected
constructed_url = base_url + path + params
headers = {
    'Ocp-Apim-Subscription-Key': subscriptionKey,
    'Content-type': 'application/json',
    'X-ClientTraceId': str(uuid.uuid4())
}
body = [{
    'text' : 'Hello world!'
}]
request = requests.post(constructed_url, headers=headers, json=body)
response = request.json()
print(json.dumps(response, sort_keys=True, indent=4, ensure_ascii=False,
    separators=(',', ': ')))
```

This code defines a subscriptionKey variable and constructs a URL variable for the translation service using Cognitive API version 3.0, with the parameter to=es, which indicates to translate the text to Spanish. Then you define a header object using your subscription key, which authenticates calls to the service. The body of the call contains the text to be sent for translation. The request is then constructed with the URL, headers, and body, and a call to request.json() to invoke the service. The response is finally printed with some formatting to make it easier to read.

On the command line, type the following to run this code:

```
python translate.py
```

After a few seconds, you should see the following:

```
[
    {
        "detectedLanguage": {
            "language": "en",
            "score": 1.0
        },
        "translations": [
            {
                "text": ";¡Hola mundo!",
                "to": "es"
            }
        ]
    }
]
```

The service has automatically detected that the source language is English and has translated it to Spanish, as expected.

Using a Cognitive Service from a Serverless Azure Functions Project

To create a serverless function, follow the steps in Chapter 4 to create a base Python Azure Functions Project. After you have created and activated the Python virtual environment and created the Functions Project, you must add the libraries that you are going to need by installing `requests` and `uuid`:

```
python -m pip install requests uuid
```

Then, create a new function with an HTTP Request trigger using `func new`. Name it `translate`, and then change the template of the code. Instead of printing a "Hello <name>" message, it will translate the text parameter that is passed in the URL:

```
import logging
import os, requests, uuid, json
import azure.functions as func
def main(req: func.HttpRequest) -> func.HttpResponse:
    logging.info('Python HTTP trigger function processed a request.')
    text = req.params.get('text')
    if not text:
        try:
            req_body = req.get_json()
        except ValueError:
            pass
        else:
            text = req_body.get('text')
    if text:
        subscriptionKey = 'e8a02b210157478a82b883af591dc599'
        base_url = 'https://api.cognitive.microsofttranslator.com'
        path = '/translate?api-version=3.0'
        params = '&to=es'
        constructed_url = base_url + path + params
        headers = {
```

```
            'Ocp-Apim-Subscription-Key': subscriptionKey,
            'Content-type': 'application/json',
            'X-ClientTraceId': str(uuid.uuid4())
        }
        body = [{
            'text' : 'Hello world!'
        }]
        request = requests.post(constructed_url, headers=headers, json=body)
        response = request.json()
        print(json.dumps(response, sort_keys=True, indent=4, ensure_ascii=False,
            separators=(',', ': ')))
        return func.HttpResponse(f"Translation: {response}!")
    else:
        return func.HttpResponse(
                "Please pass a text on the query string or in the request body",
                status_code=400
        )
```

Everything is ready! You can now run your Function App by using func host start and visit it via the function URL in your browser with the text parameter (the %20 encodes a space in the text for URLs):

```
http://localhost:7071/api/translate?text=Hello%20world!
```

You should see all of the response object details in your browser:

```
Translation: [{'detectedLanguage': {'language': 'en', 'score': 1.0},
    'translations': [{'text': '¡Hola mundo!', 'to': 'es'}]}]!
```

You now have a Functions Project that you can deploy to a Function App and start using as a serverless cognitive service for text translation.

General Machine Learning Tools, Libraries, and Frameworks

Let's learn more about machine learning tools, libraries, and frameworks. This is an advanced topic, but if your knowledge of machine learning models is not yet all that extensive, don't worry. The idea here is simply to present the tools to you so that you can recognize them when needed.

Microsoft Cognitive Toolkit

The Microsoft Cognitive Toolkit is a deep learning toolkit that describes neural networks as a series of tools to work with deep learning models and algorithms. It provides speed, scalability, and commercial-grade quality. It is open source and all the code and documentation is hosted on GitHub. It was previously referred to by the acronym CNTK, and you might still find references to that name in older documentation.

You can use Microsoft Cognitive Toolkit with the Python, C#, C++, and BrainScript programming languages. You can also use it with *Keras*, a user-friendly library to standardize configuration of different machine learning and deep learning models; all of the configuration is done at Keras level, and Microsoft Cognitive Toolkit runs in the backend. Other possibilities are to host it on the Azure Portal or use it from a Docker container image.

 You can read more about Microsoft Cognitive Toolkit at *https://www.microsoft.com/en-us/cognitive-toolkit/*.

Microsoft Cognitive Toolkit describes a neural network as a series of computational steps via a directed graph. The leaf nodes represent input values or network parameters, whereas other nodes represent matrix operations on those inputs. With Microsoft Cognitive Toolkit, you can combine model types like *feed-forward deep neural networks* (DNNs), *convolutional neural networks* (CNNs), and *recurrent neural networks/long short-term memory networks* (RNNs/LSTMs). It implements *stochastic gradient descent* (SGD, error backpropagation) learning with automatic differentiation and parallelization that can be computed across multiple graphics processing units (GPUs) and servers.

The best place to begin looking for code examples is the documentation (*https://docs.microsoft.com/en-us/cognitive-toolkit/*), which hosts many code samples, recipes, and tutorials. In addition to a "Getting Started" guide with basic explanations on how to start using Microsoft Cognitive Toolkit, you will find examples for working with the following and more:

Images
Models for image classification, generation of images, object detection, image recognition, and several other tasks related to image processing and alteration

Numeric data
Tutorials on data classification, logistic regression, time series prediction, and general forecasting of numeric data

Speech
Several models for speech recognition and grapheme to phoneme translation

Text
Tutorials on document similarity comparison, word prediction, classification, and translation from one domain (grapheme) to another (phoneme)

Reinforcement Learning
Models for training an agent to play some simple computer video games

Microsoft Cognitive Toolkit is not difficult to use in your programs, but you do need background knowledge in neural networks and machine learning to determine the best model type or algorithm and how to parametrize it to solve the real-life problem that you're working on.

You can deploy a Cognitive Toolkit model to an Azure Web App in the Azure Portal (*http://bit.ly/2GdpaXf*) and take advantage of the computing power of Microsoft's cloud.

ML.NET

ML.NET (*https://dotnet.microsoft.com/apps/machinelearning-ai/ml-dotnet*) is another framework from Microsoft, targeted specifically at .NET developers who use languages like C# and F#. It is used for building models for *regression, classification,* and *clustering*. ML.NET is cross-platform and open source and hosted on GitHub. As of this writing, it is still in preview, but its development is quite advanced.

If you are a Python developer, you are out of luck here; ML.NET is designed from the ground up for .NET programming languages.

With ML.NET you can work on many types of problems, including:

Sentiment analysis
Analyze the sentiment of customer reviews using a binary classification algorithm.

Product recommendation
Recommend products based on purchase history using a matrix factorization algorithm.

Price prediction
Predict taxi fares based on distance traveled and so on, using a regression algorithm.

Customer segmentation
Identify groups of customers with similar profiles using a clustering algorithm.

GitHub labeler
Suggest the GitHub label for new issues using a multiclass classification algorithm.

Fraud detection
Detect fraudulent credit card transactions using a binary classification algorithm.

Spam detection
Flag text messages as spam using a binary classification algorithm.

Image classification
Classify images (e.g., broccoli versus pizza) using a TensorFlow deep learning algorithm.

Sales forecasting
Forecast future sales for products using a regression algorithm.

 To learn more information about all the namespaces this framework has available to use in your projects, visit the ML.NET API Reference (*http://bit.ly/2IwBVib*).

Jupyter Notebook

Jupyter Notebook (*https://jupyter.org/*) is an open source web application that data scientists can use to create and share documents with live code, visualizations, equations, and narrative text that is human-readable. It supports more than 40 programming languages, including Python, R, Julia, and Scala, and is a very practical way to write samples and tutorials for machine learning libraries. This tool is widely used by data scientists as a high-level integrated development environment (IDE) as well as for sharing results.

TensorFlow

TensorFlow (*https://www.tensorflow.org*) is an open source programming library for symbolic math that is used for machine learning applications such as neural networks. It is based on the dataflow programming paradigm that models a program as a *directed graph* of the data flowing between operations. TensorFlow is written in a combination of highly optimized C++ and CUDA (NVIDIA's language for programming GPUs); however, it is commonly accessed through its Python API library.

You can install TensorFlow with a Python API by using Python's `pip` package manager or run it from a Docker image. In addition, you can use it from Java, C, Go, or JavaScript APIs, and there are also native ports to the JavaScript (*TensorFlow.js*) and Swift programming languages.

TensorFlow has several advantages over other tools for developing neural networks, an important one being that TensorFlow scripts can run on either a CPU or a GPU without code changes. Also, with TensorFlow you avoid one of the most tedious tasks when programing with neural networks: implementing the backpropagation algorithm (in fact, backpropagation is done by computing the derivatives numerically from previous iterations, which is more efficient).

An easy way to learn how to use TensorFlow is by visiting the Colaboratory website (*http://bit.ly/2XaicJn*), a Google Colab project using Jupyter Notebooks.

TensorFlow includes the Keras library natively and you can find many TensorFlow Keras guides in the documentation for tasks such as the following:

- Basic classification
- Text classification
- Regression
- Overfitting and underfitting
- Save and load operations

Keras

Keras (*https://keras.io/*) is a Python deep learning library that acts as a high-level neural networks API capable of running on top of TensorFlow, Microsoft Cognitive Toolkit, or Theano (for processing multidimensional arrays).

Keras allows for easy and fast prototyping, modularity, and easy extensibility. If you want to quickly build and test neural networks with minimal code, Keras is your friend.

A Keras module creation and training example can be coded in just a few lines:

```
model = Sequential()
model.add(Dense(32, activation='relu', input_dim=100))
model.add(Dense(1, activation='sigmoid'))
model.compile(optimizer='rmsprop',
              loss='binary_crossentropy',
              metrics=['accuracy'])
# Generate dummy data
import numpy as np
data = np.random.random((1000, 100))
labels = np.random.randint(2, size=(1000, 1))
# Train the model, iterating on the data in batches of 32 samples
model.fit(data, labels, epochs=10, batch_size=32)
```

Scikit-learn

Scikit-learn (*https://scikit-learn.org/stable/*) is an open source Python library for data mining and data analysis that is built on top of other libraries like NumPy, SciPy, and Matplotlib. It features various classification, regression, and clustering algorithms, including support vector machines, random forests, gradient boosting, *k*-means, and DBSCAN.

The main advantage of scikit-learn compared to other tools is that it has a soft learning curve and its syntax is oriented to machine learning rather than pure programming. It has models for every kind of machine learning problem to solve (clustering, classifying, regression, etc.).

Following is an example classifier model for handwritten digit images:

```
from sklearn import datasets, svm, metrics

# The digits dataset
digits = datasets.load_digits()
n_samples = len(digits.images)
data = digits.images.reshape((n_samples, -1))

# Create a classifier: a support vector classifier
classifier = svm.SVC(gamma=0.001)

# We learn the digits on the first half of the dataset
classifier.fit(data[:n_samples // 2], digits.target[:n_samples // 2])

# Now we predict the value of the digit on the second half
expected = digits.target[n_samples // 2:]
predicted = classifier.predict(data[n_samples // 2:])


# Results:
print("Confusion matrix:\n%s" % metrics.confusion_matrix(expected, predicted))
```

MNIST Dataset

To be able to train and validate a model for any machine learning task, we need sample data. A typical example to practice using machine learning libraries and frameworks is the Modified National Institute of Standards and Technology (MNIST) dataset. Consisting of images of handwritten digits from 0 to 9, the dataset is used in many examples for training a model to recognize handwritten text.

The dataset contains 60,000 examples for training and 10,000 examples for testing. Digits have been size-normalized and centered in a fixed-size image of 28×28 pixels. It is publicly available at *http://yann.lecun.com/exdb/mnist*.

> ### ONNX
>
> Open Neural Network Exchange (ONNX) is an open format to represent deep learning models that makes it possible to move models between different machine learning tools. You can train models in one framework and then transfer them to another for inference.
>
> The following tools support ONNX models:
>
> - Microsoft Cognitive Toolkit
> - MXNet
> - Caffe2
> - PyTorch
> - Windows Machine Learning

Cloud Machine Learning Solutions with Azure

Let's explore a couple of important tools that you can use to train and implement machine learning models in the cloud: Machine Learning Studio and Azure Machine Learning service and SDK.

Microsoft Machine Learning Studio

Machine Learning Studio is a browser-based, visual drag-and-drop authoring environment for which no coding is necessary. You can use it to build powerful projects in a simple way.

As Figure 5-1 demonstrates, with Machine Learning Studio you can perform several activities related to data science, including:

Data exploration
    Gathering information from larger unstructured datasets

Data mining
    Discovering patterns in large datasets

Descriptive analytics
    Analyzing a dataset to summarize what happened over time

Predictive analytics
    Building models to predict future outcomes

Supervised learning
    Training algorithms with labeled data

Unsupervised learning
Using unlabeled data to find possible relationships

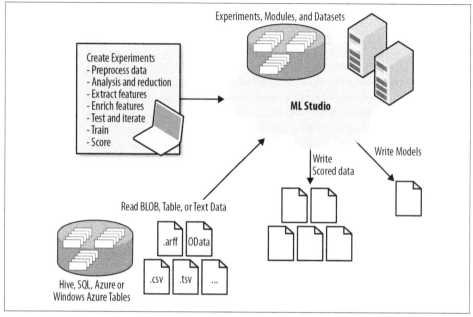

Figure 5-1. Machine Learning Studio input, outputs, and activities

In this section, we define the following application options:

Project
A concept that encapsulates a group of experiments, datasets, notebooks, and other resources representing a single project

Experiments
Experiments that you have created and run or saved as drafts

Web services
Web services that you have deployed from your experiments

Notebooks
Jupyter notebooks that you have created

Datasets
Datasets that you have uploaded into Machine Learning Studio

Trained models
Models that you have trained in experiments and saved in Machine Learning Studio

Settings

A collection of settings that you can use to configure your account and resources

Launch Azure Machine Learning Studio, and in the bar at the bottom, click the NEW button. A dialog box opens that presents you with several options:

Dataset

Import your own dataset.

Module

Import a module from a ZIP package or choose one from the Azure AI Gallery.

Project

Create a new empty project.

Experiment

Create a new empty experiment, or run the experiment tutorial or any of the experiments in the Azure AI Gallery.

Notebook

Search any AI Notebooks from the Azure AI Gallery.

Creating a predictive example that can be invoked from a serverless app

Now, let's create and train a model that will be able to predict a person's expected income based on several key parameters.

Here are the steps to create a new experiment:

1. In Machine Learning Studio, in the menu bar at the bottom of the window, click the NEW button, and then select Experiment. You can click on the automatically generated experiment name to change it.

2. In the upper left of the window, use the "Search experiment items" search box to look for a dataset.

3. Type **Income**, and then drag and drop "Adult census income binary" into your experiment area.

4. Click the lower point of the block (output) to open a window that shows a review of the data you added.

5. Now you need to split this dataset so that you can use part of it for training a model, and another part to validate the training.

6. Search again for Split, and then add a Split Data block. Leave it with its default properties.

7. Select a machine learning model to train. Search for Two-Class, and then drag Two-Class Boosted Decision Tree to your experiment.

8. Search for and add a Train Model block to your experiment.

9. Connect the model and the first Split Data output to the Train Model inputs.

10. Click this block, and then, on the right side, select the "Launch column selector" option and specify to use the "income" column.

11. Add a Score Model that takes the Train Model and second Split Data outputs as inputs, and then add an Evaluate Model block and connect its first input to the Score Model output.

12. Run the experiment and train the model by clicking the RUN button in the bottom bar.

The process takes several seconds; a green checkmark displays on the right side of each block as it finishes processing. Then, when you click the output point of Evaluate Model, a Visualization window opens, as shown in Figure 5-2, presenting graphical and tabular data on the results of the training.

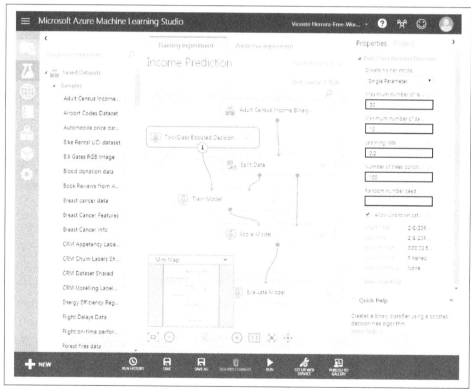

Figure 5-2. Training model data workflow in Azure Machine Learning Studio

To use this trained model with the pretrained Cognitive Services models that you explored earlier, you need to set it up as a web service. Here's how to do that:

1. In the menu bar at the bottom, click DEPLOY WEB SERVICE.

   A new tab named "Predictive experiment" will appear at the top of your experiment, leaving the previous work in a "Training experiment" tab. "Web service input" and "Web service output" are added to the database.

2. Add a "Select Columns in Dataset" block that connects the Adult Census Income Binary Data and the Score Model at the second input (the same that "Web service input" is using).

3. Click the "Select Columns in Database" block, and then, on the right tab, select "Launch column selector" and type "Income."

4. Place another "Select Columns in Dataset" block between the Score Model and "Web service output" blocks, as shown in Figure 5-3, replacing their current connection, and then select the Scored Labels and Scored Probabilities columns.

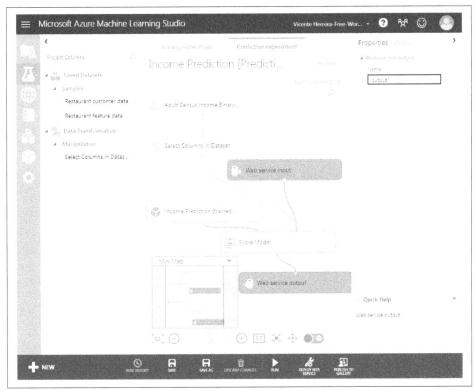

Figure 5-3. The predictive experiment in Azure Machine Learning Studio

Your model is now ready to deploy. In the menu bar at the bottom of the window, click DEPLOY WEB SERVICE. Your view will change, and the "Web services" icon will be selected on the left instead of the Experiment icon. Here, you can view general information like the API key to access this service, a snapshot and the latest version of the published experiment, and the endpoints. Click any of these to see more detailed documentation:

Request/Response
    The endpoint to invoke for a single prediction execution

Batch Execution
    The endpoint to use for processing a series of data

Deploying to the Edge

Azure IoT Edge is a managed service that you can use to deploy code that implements functionality on your IoT Edge devices. The idea is to use your IoT devices as a computation platform; that is, with IoT Edge you can manage your code as a cloud service, but instead of running on the Azure platform it runs on your IoT devices, directly using sensors to obtain the data that is quickly processed within them. You can use this as a target deployment for Azure Machine Learning service and for some Azure Cognitive Services, like Custom Vision.

Azure Machine Learning Service

Azure Machine Learning service (*https://azure.microsoft.com/en-us/services/machine-learning-service*) provides a cloud-based environment in which you can develop, train, test, deploy, and manage machine learning models. You can think of it as an alternative to Machine Learning Studio that uses code to describe your machine learning project instead of visual blocks.

Azure Machine Learning service supports several open source frameworks, such as PyTorch, TensorFlow, scikit-learn, CNTK, and MXNet, as well as thousands of other open source Python packages with machine learning components.

You can begin training your model on your local machine and then scale out to the Azure cloud. Azure Machine Learning service incorporates DevOps capabilities for machine learning that provide an improvement on productivity for managing models in the cloud.

Here are some of the advantages of using Azure Machine Learning service:

- SDK for Python as well as Jupyter Notebook tool
- Automated model generation, training, and tuning

- Cloud-scale models trained from local machine
- Easy integration into a container to deploy elsewhere (Azure Kubernetes Service, Azure Container Instances, on premises, etc.)

Main components

Let's begin to explain some of the terminology that we use to program a project for Azure Machine Learning service:

Model
A piece of code that takes input and produces output that is run by Azure Machine Learning service. It is agnostic to the framework (scikit-learn, Tensor-Flow, Microsoft Cognitive Toolkit, etc.). It keeps track of all the models in your Azure Machine Learning service workspace.

Deployment
An instance of an image with a model application and its dependencies. It can be served through Azure Container Instances or Azure Kubernetes Service with a load balancer or HTTP endpoint. You can also deploy model images to devices by using Azure IoT Edge on edge devices.

Datastore
A storage abstraction over Azure that is used to retrieve data (Azure Blob Storage or Azure Files).

Run
An execution of the model produced when you submit a script to train a model. A run can have zero or more child runs. The group of runs from a specified script is called an *experiment*. The infrastructure resource used by the runs is known as the *compute target*.

Pipeline
An object that creates and manages workflows that stitch together machine learning phases. Each phase can encompass multiple steps, each of which can run unattended in various compute targets.

Azure Machine Learning software development kit

You can install in your local environment the Python software development kit (SDK) to work with all the resources from the Azure Machine Learning SDK as a client from your machine. Key functional capabilities of the SDK include the following:

- Managing cloud resources for monitoring, logging, and organizing experiments
- Training models either locally or using cloud resources

- Using automated machine learning, which accepts configuration parameters and training data, and automatically iterates through algorithms and hyperparameter settings to find the best model for running predictions

- Deploying web services to convert your trained models into RESTful services that can be consumed in any application

TensorFlow models and the Azure Machine Learning SDK

The Azure Machine Learning SDK provides a custom TensorFlow that enables you to easily submit TensorFlow training jobs for both single-node and distributed runs on Azure compute.

Azure Machine Learning supports two methods of distributed training in Tensor-Flow:

- MPI-based distributed training using the Horovod framework
- Native distributed TensorFlow via the parameter server method

Another alternative is using Keras within the Azure Machine Learning SDK, which can be a more approachable way of using TensorFlow.

 You can find more detailed information in the Azure Machine Learning SDK for Python documentation (*http://bit.ly/2IuoVts*).

Azure Machine Learning for Visual Studio Code

Azure Machine Learning for Visual Studio Code (*https://docs.microsoft.com/en-us/azure/machine-learning/service/how-to-vscode-tools*) is an extension to help you work using this editor with machine learning and deep learning projects. You can use it with Microsoft Cognitive Toolkit, TensorFlow, and other deep learning frameworks. It connects to Azure Machine Learning service to help you prepare data, train models, and deploy machine learning models to the Azure Portal at the Azure Machine Learning service.

Using Azure Machine Learning for Visual Studio Code, which you can see in Figure 5-4, you can benefit from the usual features like syntax highlighting, Intelli-Sense (autocompletion), and text autoformatting, specifically for the Azure Machine Learning SDK. You can use it to debug by setting up breakpoints to stop the execution of your projects when you run them in your local environment.

Figure 5-4. Azure Machine Learning for Visual Studio Code

You will also find an Azure AI Gallery browser and tools to submit jobs to the Azure cloud or to different compute targets like Spark clusters, Azure GPU virtual machines, and more.

> The Visual Studio Code extension for Azure Machine Learning is available in the Visual Studio Marketplace (*http://bit.ly/2v3lgeh*).

Visual Studio Tools for AI

You can find a separate tool called Visual Studio Tools for AI, which is meant not for the "Code" variant that shares its name but the original Visual Studio, for which you can also try the Express edition. It is similar in scope to Azure Machine Learning for Visual Studio Code but developed for the original Visual Studio IDE. Again, this is different from the far more streamlined Code variant of the IDE.

> You can learn more about Visual Studio Tools for AI on the Microsoft website (*http://bit.ly/2Uzyv5m*).

Data Science Virtual Machines

Data Science Virtual Machines (*http://bit.ly/2Z84U1z*) is an Azure Virtual Machines service that facilitates preconfigured virtual machines (VMs) for data science modeling, development, and deployment. You will find VMs for several programming languages as well as tools for development, deep learning, machine learning, data exploration, and visualization, and data platform and ingestion tools.

Azure Virtual Machines offers a "pay as you go" model in the same line as serverless architecture as well as "reserved virtual machines instances," for an advanced purchase of a VM for one or three years.

Azure Notebooks

Azure Notebooks (*https://notebooks.azure.com*) is a Jupyter Notebooks implementation hosted for Azure project information. It implements examples in the Python 2, Python 3, R, and F# programming languages.

You can find several examples of Azure Machine Learning service notebooks on the website (*https://notebooks.azure.com/azureml/projects/azureml-getting-started*).

## PART III

Deployment and Continuous Delivery

## CHAPTER 6

Deployment and Scaling

After you develop a first version of any application, you need to deploy it to the infrastructure on which it will run.

By their very nature, serverless applications do not have an issue with scaling. But it is also true that an event-driven serverless project usually relies on many services that your cloud environment provides. For cases in which you need a more tailored setup, Kubernetes gives you a way to configure your customized containers to your needs. In this chapter, we explain how to use Azure Kubernetes Service (AKS) to orchestrate your custom containers.

Deployment Options

Deploying your Function App from the command line, as we have done so far, is just the first way to put your development on the Azure infrastructure. Sadly, as Python language support is in preview as of this writing, we must rely on this single method for deployment: a custom container to compile your Python code with all the virtual environment requirements is needed. But for a Function App in any other programming language, we have multiple options that we explain here so that you can take advantage of the concepts as soon as they become available for Python.

On your Function App web page in the Azure Portal, where all the contents and options are displayed, click the Platform Features tab. Then, in the "Code deployment" section, click the "Deployment center" link. When you visit it, several source control options are available, including a number of locations from which you can pull code:

Azure Repos
  Configure continuous integration with an Azure Repo, part of Azure DevOps Services (formerly known as Visual Studio Team Services, or VSTS).

GitHub
> Configure continuous integration with a GitHub repository.

Bitbucket
> Configure continuous integration with a Bitbucket repository.

Local Git
> Deploy from a local Git repository.

OneDrive
> Synchronize content from a OneDrive cloud folder.

Dropbox
> Synchronize content from a Dropbox cloud folder.

External
> Deploy from a public Git or Mercurial repository.

FTP
> Use an FTP connection to access and copy app files.

If you use Azure Repos, GitHub, or Bitbucket, you will be asked to provide credentials to access the service. To set up the deployment options, choose from among the existing repositories. A remote origin should be added to that repository so that when you push content to it, it is received on the pipeline and triggers the deployment automation. We do not recommend using a OneDrive, Dropbox, or FTP connection for deployment, because they do not provide real version control for your files and will try to deploy any associated synchronization to them.

After you have selected the source control platform, you need to specify what build provider to use:

App Service Kudu build server
> This engine automatically builds your code during deployment when applicable, with no additional configuration required.

Azure Pipelines (in preview)
> Using this engine, you can configure a custom deployment pipeline for your application that builds, runs load tests on, and deploys your app.

Choosing the first option allows you to do everything automatically and finish setting up the deployment configuration.

If you select the second option, an additional staging environment will be available for configuration, which allows you to customize the entire workflow for deployment even further using the Azure DevOps service.

You then are asked whether you want to create a new DevOps organization and project or specify an existing one, as illustrated in Figure 6-1. For the Function App Type, you should choose Script Function App, unless you are using a .NET language that you want to deploy as a precompiled package. You can leave Working Directory blank.

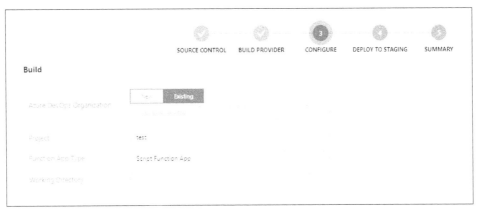

Figure 6-1. Configuring an environment using Azure Pipelines (preview)

In the final step, you are asked whether you would like to set up a "development slot" that will be allocated in the same Function App. This allows you to differentiate between calls on that slot and those on the main version of the application. This is a useful way to test your app thoroughly before deploying a release version.

Azure DevOps

This service has its own URL at *https://dev.azure.com*, and you should visit it to create a new *organization* so that you can add *projects* to it. On the main Azure Portal site, you can read properties only for already existing DevOps organizations.

With Azure DevOps, you can create and manage DevOps organizations and projects, customize pipelines for deploying, and use other project management tools, including the following:

Dashboards
    You can add widgets for quick access to history, charts for test plans, work items, sprint burndown, and many other options.

Wiki
    A collaborative documentation space for the project.

Boards
    Agile and Scrum boards to track tasks.

Repositories

The source code repositories associated with the projects.

Pipelines

You can set up the pipelines to automate code and artifact acquisition, testing, and deployment using a GUI and many preconfigured templates.

Test plans

You can create test from cards on boards, using a browser extension or the advanced module Test Manager extension.

Artifacts

Maven, npm, and NuGet packages from public and private sources that you share with your team.

Figure 6-2 demonstrates that with pipelines, you have a graphical tool that lets you set up source code to be pushed to a branch in the repository (using Artifacts definition). This code can trigger one or more jobs that can be target deployments or tests that should be passed before the deployment is automatically triggered.

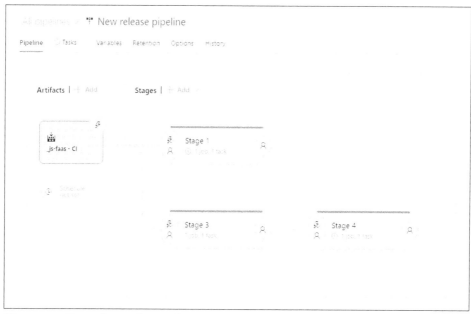

Figure 6-2. Using the pipeline tool in Azure DevOps

Figure 6-3 shows how new tasks are created from a list of many different templates. In this example, we have selected the one for deploying a Function App to Azure Functions.

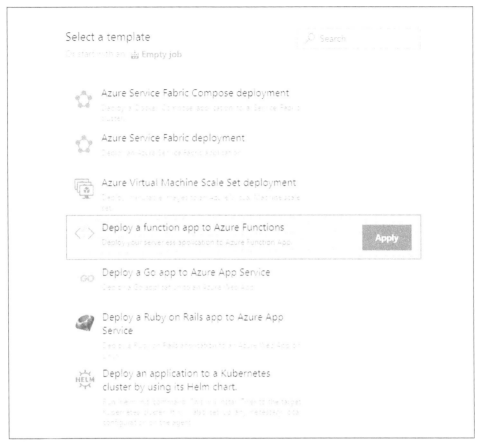

Figure 6-3. Selecting a template in Azure DevOps

Docker

Docker is a lightweight virtualization tool that you can use as a platform to develop, deploy, and run containerized applications. The philosophy of Docker is to virtualize processes, not systems. This is because Docker only virtualizes the software (and in fact not all the software) and skips the hardware virtualization as a way of saving resources. Many people are comfortable using Docker to launch their projects, so we'll just go through a bit of how-to here.

For instance, suppose that you wanted to containerize a Python sklearn application that is in */app* and is executed by running a script called *model.py*. You would need to build an image with Python and sklearn (you can get a prebuilt one from the Docker public repository, Docker Hub) and then put your code inside the image with the Dockerfile.

To do that, you must assemble some commands in a Dockerfile and build it. To run it, at the command line, type the following:

```
docker build -t model_image -f Dockerfile
docker run model_image
```

The Dockerfile is a file that contains a sequence of commands that instruct Docker how to build an image. In this case, the Dockerfile would look like this (`alpine-python-machinelearning` is a Python image with sklearn prebuilt):

```
FROM frolvlad/alpine-python-machinelearning
COPY ./model.py /model.py
RUN python model.py
```

All data from a container is lost when the running app exits, whatever the reason (even if the program finishes successfully). In the area of machine learning, when your model finishes, you might want keep whatever data it generates (the trained model in a training process, the prediction in an inferencing model, etc.). To prevent this loss of data, Docker uses the concept of *volumes*.

A volume is a mechanism to save data safely outside of the container while at the same time making it accessible from within the container as if it were a native file. To start a container with a volume that does not yet exist, Docker creates the volume for you by executing the `docker run` of a built image, as follows:

```
docker run --mount source=my_vol,target=<DIR_PATH> model_image
```

Azure Container Registry

Storing the images in a cloud repository is useful to preserve and share them. You can do this with Docker by using the `push` command (sometimes the name of the image needs to have a specific format). For instance, to push an image to Azure Container Registry you can run the following:

```
az acr login --name <MY_REGISTRY>
docker tag my_image <MY_REGISTRY>.azurecr.io/my_image
docker push <MY_REGISTRY>.azurecr.io/my_image
```

Azure Container Registry is not only a Docker image repository; it can also build the images for you without the need of having Docker locally installed. The are other tools that go a step further and let you run the images, such as Azure Container Instance, but in this case we don't need that.

From a data scientist's perspective, it might be interesting to run this process as a service that can be invoked from outside the container to enable predictions with new data in a development environment. With Python, you can do this with the Flask library after opening its service port so that it is reachable from outside.

The main advantage of Docker in this context is that it gives your application full compatibility with most systems due to virtualization, and at the same time it is very easy to configure. Moreover, it is also very likely that the image that you need already exists in the official public Docker repository, Docker Hub (*https://hub.docker.com/*).

Kubernetes

Even though you can run an application in a single Docker container, that is not going to be enough for a real application. For complex systems, applications are separated into several containers, with each of them running different parts.

Using Docker to split and run applications makes it possible to scale them efficiently. Beyond that, we also want to build in redundancy so that in case there is a failure in one node, the entire system will keep working in a production environment. Kubernetes is the way to implement this.

Kubernetes is a software tool to orchestrate Docker images across a distributed cluster. In contrast with other image management tools, Kubernetes has proven high availability (HA) and serves a production-ready development environment.

Regarding machine learning benefits, Kubernetes also has tools to develop and train algorithms simultaneously with popular frameworks such as TensorFlow. There are also convenient Kubernetes extensions (Custom Resources) for machine learning, such as TFJob and JupyterHub (we talk more about both later in the chapter).

The other main benefit of Kubernetes is the easy distribution processing. With Azure Kubernetes Service a data scientist can have a Kubernetes cluster ready to use in minutes and with a cost that always will be less than the cost of having physical machines with the same properties on premises. For instance, creating a minimal Kubernetes cluster in Azure is as simple as executing this command:

```
az aks create \
    --resource-group <RESOURCE_GROUP> \
    --name <CLUSTER_NAME> \
    --node-count 1 \
    --generate-ssh-keys
```

Kubernetes resources

Kubernetes has many different resources that can be helpful when deploying an app. The resources that we discuss in this section are the following:

Pods
> The smallest and simplest Kubernetes object. A Pod represents a single container or a set of running containers on your cluster. This is the basic unit for all of the workloads you run on Kubernetes.

Deployment

The most common way of running *multiple* copies (Pods) of your application. It supports rolling updates to your container images.

Service

By itself, a Deployment can't receive traffic. Setting up a Service is one of the simplest ways to configure a Deployment to receive and balance requests.

The resources in Kubernetes are custom-deployed by the user via files called *configuration files* or *manifests*. These files are in YAML or JSON format with a determined structure according to the resource being described and in terms of Kubernetes API object. Here's an example of a configuration file for a Pod:

```
apiVersion: v1
kind: Pod
metadata:
  name: my_pod
spec:
  containers:
  - name: my_pod
    image: <MY_REGISTRY>.azurecr.io/my_image
    resources:
      limits:
        cpu: 100m
        memory: 128Mi
      limits:
        cpu: 250m
        memory: 256Mi
```

In the same way as Docker containers, Pods lose their data when they cease to exist or die. The solution that Kubernetes provides is also to configure an external storage through the API extensions `PersistentVolume` and `PersistentVolumeClaim`.

If multiple Pods need concurrent access to the same storage volume, you can use the Azure Files or Azure Disk Storage services to connect to them using the Server Message Block (SMB) protocol with a static or dynamic space.

For the simplest case, you need only to create an Azure Files static space. First, create the Resource Group and storage account:

```
az group create --name <RESOURCE_GROUP> --location <LOCATION>
az storage account create -n <STORAGE_ACCOUNT> -g \
<RESOURCE_GROUP> -l <LOCATION> --sku Standard_LRS
```

Then export the connection string and create the file share:

```
export CONNECTION=`az storage account show-connection-string \
-n <STORAGE_ACCOUNT> -g <RESOURCE_GROUP> -o tsv`
az storage share create -n <SHARE_NAME>
```

Kubernetes needs credentials to access Azure Files. The way to give Kubernetes access to Azure is through a Kubernetes Secret. To use this, you need the `kubectl` client, as shown in the following commands:

```
STORAGE_KEY=$(az storage account keys list \
  --resource-group <RESOURCE_GROUP> \
  --account-name <STORAGE_ACCOUNT> \
  --query "[0].value" -o tsv)
kubectl create secret generic azure-secret \
  --from-literal=azurestorageaccountname=<STORAGE_ACCOUNT> \
  --from-literal=azurestorageaccountkey=$STORAGE_KEY
```

Now you just need to modify the YAML of the Pod to mount the Azure Files share into it, in the path specified in the field `mountPath`:

```
apiVersion: v1
kind: Pod
metadata:
  name: my_pod
spec:
  containers:
  - name: my_pod
    image: <MY_REGISTRY>.azurecr.io/my_image
    resources:
      limits:
        cpu: 100m
        memory: 128Mi
      limits:
        cpu: 250m
        memory: 256Mi
    volumeMounts:
      - name: azure_volume
        mountPath: /mnt/data
  volumes:
  - name: azure_volume
    azureFile:
      secretName: azure-secret
      shareName: <SHARE_NAME>
      readOnly: false
```

Kubernetes scalability—virtual nodes

The advantage of a Kubernetes cluster in the cloud is that you can easily scale up your resources manually whenever you want, just by updating the cluster configuration. This can take a few minutes, depending on the number of nodes you want to scale. It's as easy as doing the following:

```
az aks scale \
  --resource-group <RESOURCE_GROUP> \
  --name <CLUSTER_NAME> \
  --node-count 1 \
  --nodepool-name <your node pool name>
```

Cloud Kubernetes services usually give you the choice of autoscaling, too. This autoscaling is done by generating new Pods when the service demand requires it, and generating new nodes when the cluster can't be scheduled on nodes because of resource constraints. In Azure you can reconfigure your cluster to autoscale by using the following:

```
az aks update \
  --resource-group <RESOURCE_GROUP> \
  --name <CLUSTER_NAME> \
  --enable-cluster-autoscaler \
  --min-count 1 \
  --max-count 3
```

One interesting tool available in Azure (that currently is in preview) is virtual nodes. Virtual nodes allow you to elastically provision additional Pods inside Container Instances that start in seconds.

Machine Learning Tools for Kubernetes

Managing a Kubernetes cluster for machine learning on its own is not a simple task. We can use several tools like Kubeflow, ksonnet and kubectl to make it easier.

Kubeflow

Whether you are a data scientist preparing your own infrastructure or a DevOp preparing a platform for a data scientist team, you might not want to implement by hand all of the details for the management of the job distribution over containers and nodes. Your focus is on how to set up the data pipeline process when developing and training your model.

Kubeflow is an open source project dedicated to providing easy-to-use machine learning resources on top of a Kubernetes cluster, making running a machine learning workload on Kubernetes simple, portable, and scalable. You can deploy Kubeflow in Kubernetes as a ksonnet app (see "ksonnet" on page 104), as shown here:

```
ks registry add kubeflow github.com/kubeflow/kubeflow/tree/v0.2.2/kubeflow
```

From the point of view of Kubernetes, the installation of Kubeflow involves only the deployment of different resources in the cluster to assist with a variety of tasks, all of them related to the machine learning process. For instance, if you run kubectl get pods after installing Kubeflow, you will get the following output:

```
NAME                                   READY  STATUS   RESTARTS  AGE
ambassador-849fb9c8c5-4v79h            2/2    Running  0         6s
ambassador-849fb9c8c5-9zs5p            2/2    Running  0         6s
ambassador-849fb9c8c5-lxjzg            2/2    Running  0         6s
centraldashboard-5d8d6ccdf8-cf547      1/1    Running  0         6s
tf-hub-0                               1/1    Running  0         6s
```

```
tf-job-dashboard-bfc9bc6bc-rwc6q          1/1    Running    0    6s
tf-job-operator-v1alpha2-756cf9cb97-szk6x 1/1    Running    0    6s
```

Here, we focus on the main Kubeflow resources related to our goal of deploying a serverless machine learning solution orchestrated with Kubernetes.

Kubeflow Pipeline. The idea of Kubeflow Pipeline is to build machine learning applications oriented to what is called a *pipeline structure*. A pipeline consists of applications divided into independent containers according to functional steps that are designed to be executed sequentially following a defined graph.

For instance, a Python machine learning application is divided into modules in a structure like this:

```
/data
    ├── train.txt
    ├── test.txt
/scripts:
    ├── main.py
    ├── data_preprocess.py
    ├── train_model.py
    ├── predict_model.py
    ├── hyperparameters.py
```

With the pipeline philosophy, every *.py* file in this example could be in an independent container with its own dependencies. Instead of running them all with a *main.py* file, you create a graph with Kubeflow Pipeline to connect all the container modules sequentially.

Kubeflow Pipeline not only connects the containers, but also schedules them and provides a user interface for managing and tracking experiments, jobs, and runs. In the future, it will offer end-to-end orchestration of the containers (this is expected in the 0.4.1 release).

Kubeflow TensorFlow. There are many components that we could use to work with tasks related to TensorFlow in Kubeflow (e.g., NVIDIA TensorRT Inference Server, TensorFlow Serving, TensorFlow Batch Predict, TensorFlow Training). The intrinsic idea in all of them is to ease the issues of working with TensorFlow in a distributed cluster. This is one of the main benefits of working with TensorFlow and Kubernetes; the good integration found in Kubeflow affords all the advantages of Kubernetes—distributed processing, production-ready environment, high availability. Kubeflow is becoming available in different frameworks, such as Caffe, PyTorch, and more.

You can use these tools for developing and training a model in a distributed environment as well as to serve a trained model as a production environment.

Kubeflow JupyterHub. Kubeflow offers a component called JupyterHub, which is a Jupyter Notebook interface, so that you can execute notebooks on the Kubernetes platform. Additionally, JupyterHub is a multiuser hub, so it spawns, manages, and proxies multiple instances of the single-user Jupyter Notebook server. For these two reasons, JupyterHub is a good tool to scale notebooks across a number of machines and users working simultaneously.

You access the JupyterHub notebook through the browser with a defined host. Users can select the GPU and CPU resources, and when you log in with your user credentials, you are given a spawned instance of the notebook.

Deploying in Kubernetes.   As you have seen, you deploy the resources in Kubernetes by applying YAML or JSON files with the Kubernetes client, kubectl. If you have already done this, you will note that the majority of the YAML files for the same resources are mostly the same. But just doing a copy/paste of the skeleton and having multiple YAML versions of the same resource can be a source of errors. Luckily, there is a tool that can help: ksonnet.

ksonnet

ksonnet is a tool for deploying resources in Kubernetes. You can install it from its GitHub repository by using the following commands (in this example, for an Ubuntu machine):

```
wget -O ks.tar.gz \
    https://github.com/ksonnet/ksonnet/releases/download/v0.12.0/ \
    ks_0.12.0_linux_amd64.tar.gz
mkdir ks && tar xf ks.tar.gz -C ks --strip-components 1
sudo mv ks/ks /usr/bin/
sudo chown root:root /usr/bin/ks
sudo chmod a+x /usr/bin/ks
```

You can initiate a project with ksonnet as follows:

```
ks init project
```

This creates a file structure like this:

```
/project
├── app.yaml
├── components // What is deployed to your cluster
│   └── params.libsonnet
├── environments // Where your app is deployed
│   ├── base.libsonnet
│   └── default
│       ├── main.jsonnet
│       ├── params.libsonnet
│       └── spec.json
├── lib // Helper code specific to your app
└── vendor // External libraries that your app leverages
```

ksonnet also gathers resource configuration files according to manifests called *components*. The resources can be simple as a Pod or as complex as a complete logging stack. Components are located in the */components* folder.

Furthermore, ksonnet adds a further abstraction that is closer to the objects in object-oriented programming. Prototypes from ksonnet are preconfigured components that allow you to skip some of the tedious boilerplate setup tasks; you simply need to set some parameters for your specific app, as shown here:

```
ks prototype list
ks prototype describe redis-stateless // prebuilt prototype
ks generate redis-stateless redis
```

kubectl

Client access to Kubernetes is done using the kubectl tool. kubectl is a command-line interface for running commands against Kubernetes. Explaining kubectl in depth is beyond the scope of this book; however, it is important to mention how to create and remove resources with kubectl using their YAML configuration files, as demonstrated here:

```
kubectl apply -f ./my_pod.yaml
kubectl delete -f ./my_pod.yaml
```

You can get information about the deployed resources in Kubernetes by using the get command:

```
kubectl get pods
kubectl get services
```

Although not a good practice in Kubernetes, it is sometimes useful to connect to a container console to execute system commands, mainly to check things when something goes wrong:

```
kubectl exec -it <POD_NAME> bash
```

Single-Container Machine Learning

Using the tools described in the preceding sections, you can develop, train, serve, and test a machine learning model. The minimum machine learning service deployed in Kubernetes consists of an inference model (trained beforehand) on a single container.

This case is especially useful when you have a locally trained model that seems to work well and you want to deploy it in the context of a Kubernetes app, or even if you want to create a simple public service without much scaling potential.

The machine learning local application in this example has a file structure like this:

```
/ml_app
├── requirements.txt
├── /model
│     └── trained_model.pkl
├── /data
│     ├── train.txt
│     └── text.txt
├── train_script.py
├── predict_script.py
└── main_script.py
```

In this example, *trained_model.pkl* is a Python-readable file with the trained model, and *requirements.txt* is a file with the dependencies from Python. The files *train.py* and *predict.py* are for training and predicting, respectively, whereas *main.py* is a Flask quick-to-go web service to be posted with new data to predict:

```
import predict_script
from flask import Flask, request
app = Flask(__name__)
@app.route("/predict", method=["POST"])
def predict():
        new_data = request.data
return predict_script.model.predict(new_data)
```

We want to create a container for this app that runs *main.py* to start a web service with the trained algorithm. You can use Docker to create an image on your local machine with a Dockerfile, like this:

```
FROM frolvlad/alpine-python-machinelearning
COPY ./ml_app ./ml_app
WORKDIR "./ml_app"
RUN pip install -r requirements.txt
EXPOSE 5000
CMD FLASK_APP=main.py flask run --host=0.0.0.0
```

You create and push the image by doing the following:

```
docker build -t my_ml_image .
docker tag my_ml_image <MY_REGISTRY>.azurecr.io/my_ml_image
docker push <MY_REGISTRY>.azurecr.io/my_ml_image
```

Finally, when your image is created with your machine learning model and pushed to your repository, you need only to customize your YAML file to take the image from the repository and deploy it, as demonstrated here:

```
apiVersion: apps/v1
kind: Deployment
metadata:
  name: my_ml_image
spec:
  replicas: 3
  selector:
    matchLabels:
```

```
        app: my_ml_image
    template:
      metadata:
        labels:
          app: my_ml_image
      spec:
        containers:
        - name: my_ml_image
          image: <MY_REGISTRY>.azurecr.io/my_ml_image
          ports:
          - containerPort: 5000
```

In a real model, either the training data might change or you might want to update the image without having to rebuild it (or maybe your container is not changeable). In such cases, you should consider adding a volume into your image by editing the YAML file:

```
apiVersion: apps/v1
kind: Deployment
metadata:
  name: my_ml_image
spec:
  replicas: 3
  selector:
    matchLabels:
        app: my_ml_image
  template:
    metadata:
      labels:
        app: my_ml_image
    spec:
      containers:
      - name: my_ml_image
        image: <MY_REGISTRY>.azurecr.io/my_ml_image
        ports:
        - containerPort: 5000
      volumeMounts:
      - mountPath: ./data
        name: my_ml_image_data
    volumes:
    - name: my_ml_image_data
      azureFile:
        secretName: azure-secret
        shareName: files-kubernetes
        readOnly: false
```

With this architecture, you now have a machine learning service deployed in a Kubernetes cluster that can be called by any other Pod through the Kubernetes DNS. If accessing from other Pods is not enough and you need your machine learning service to be a public service, you'll need two more components, a Service and an Ingress.

Jupyter Notebook in Kubernetes

In this example, we look at how to quickly execute a minimal Jupyter Notebook in Kubernetes. This can be helpful to those data scientists who do not want to struggle with managing containers.

Docker Hub offers some prebuilt images with Jupyter prepared to run; you only need to apply a YAML file via `kubectl`, like this:

```
apiVersion: apps/v1
kind: Deployment
metadata:
  name: jupyter-notebook
  labels:
    app: jupyter-notebook
spec:
  replicas: 1
  selector:
    matchLabels:
      app: jupyter-notebook
  template:
    metadata:
      labels:
        app: jupyter-notebook
    spec:
      containers:
      - name: minimal-notebook
        image: jupyter/minimal-notebook:latest
        ports:
        - containerPort: 8888
```

You could easily improve this Jupyter deployment, adding a public service, password access, volumes, and so on. This example shows only a quick-to-go deployment; if you need more features, you should think about moving to JupyterHub.

Distributed Machine Learning with TFJob

To deploy a distributed TensorFlow algorithm without any helper tool is a difficult task that requires mastery of both distributed system management and neural network development. However, with the TFJob resource, you can achieve the same result just by defining some configuration files.

To be sure that you have the TFJob tool in Kubernetes, we recommend that you deploy Kubeflow. You then need to initialize your `ksonnet` application and install the Kubeflow packages.

First, initialize a `ksonnet` app and set the namespace as `default`:

```
ks init my-kubeflow
cd my-kubeflow
ks env set default --namespace my-kubeflow
```

Then add a reference to Kubeflow's ksonnet manifests and install the Kubeflow components:

```
ks registry add kubeflow github.com/kubeflow/kubeflow/tree/v0.2.2/kubeflow
ks pkg install kubeflow/core@v0.2.2
ks pkg install kubeflow/tf-serving@v0.2.2
```

Create templates for the core components, and customize Kubeflow's installation for the Azure Kubernetes Service:

```
ks generate kubeflow-core kubeflow-core
ks param set kubeflow-core cloud aks
```

Finally, deploy Kubeflow:

```
ks apply default -c kubeflow-core
```

Now you can use TFJob as a Custom Resource Definition (CRD) in your Azure Kubernetes Service. A TFJob object has many specifications that we do not cover in this book (but which you might want to investigate on your own). The main point to take into account is that TFJob not only distributes the TensorFlow process automatically, but also with a minimal change to the code where you pass to TensorFlow the cluster specification (using tf.train.ClusterSpec()) in a file usually called *TF_CONFIG*. For a cluster with one master and two workers, the code might look like this:

```
{
    "cluster":{
        "master":[
            "distributed-breast-cancer-master-5oz2-0:2222"
        ],
        "worker":[
            "distributed-breast-cancer-worker-5oz2-0:2222",
            "distributed-breast-cancer-worker-5oz2-1:2222"
        ]
    },
    "task":{
        "type":"worker",
        "index":1
    },
    "environment":"cloud"
}
```

This TFJob object demonstrates how simple TensorFlow training YAML is. We specify an NVIDIA GPU for the job and the image tf-mnist:gpu uploaded in our Azure Container Registry with a TensorFlow model running (in this instance, the MNIST model from the public examples in the repository of TensorFlow):

```
apiVersion: kubeflow.org/v1alpha2
kind: TFJob
metadata:
  name: tensorflow_module
```

```
spec:
  tfReplicaSpecs: 1
    MASTER:
      replicas: 1
      template:
        spec:
          containers:
            - image: <MY_REGISTRY>.azurecr.io/tf-mnist:gpu
              name: tensorflow
              resources:
                limits:
                  nvidia.com/gpu: 1
              volumeMounts:
                - name: azurefile
                  subPath: tensorflow_module
                  mountPath: /tmp/tensorflow
          restartPolicy: OnFailure
          volumes:
            - name: azurefile
              persistentVolumeClaim:
                claimName: azurefile
```

If you try GPU images, your cluster nodes need to have GPUs installed. This is not a problem in Azure; when you install your AKS cluster, you can configure your node to be GPU-equipped. The `persistentVolumeClaim` is a resource of Kubernetes for getting space from a dynamic storage. This storage is needed for saving the trained model.

You run the TensorFlow job by executing the following command:

```
kubectl create -f tensorflow_module.yaml.
```

This creates a TFJob resource and a Pod in your Kubernetes cluster and then runs it. When the Pod is complete, you can see the logs by running `kubectl logs` on the Pod name.

## CHAPTER 7

Security

So far, we have allocated resources and deployed endpoints for our serverless applications without paying much attention to who can access them. But when working with serverless projects, security is extremely important. Not only should you manage who has rights to access information, but you must also take into consideration the possibility of abuse, which could cause the costs of the servers to escalate proportionally to the workload unless you have established limits.

Azure Functions Authorization Levels

Our first step should be to pay a little more attention to the authorization level of our deployed functions.

When we create a new function in our Function App with the command `func new`, we can see in its *function.json* definition file that the authentication level by default is `anonymous`:

```
{
  "scriptFile": "__init__.py",
  "bindings": [
    {
      "authLevel": "anonymous",
      "type": "httpTrigger",
      "direction": "in",
      "name": "req",
      "methods": [
        "get",
        "post"
      ]
    },
    {
      "type": "http",
```

```
        "direction": "out",
        "name": "$return"
      }
    ]
  }
}
```

For any level that is not anonymous, an access key must be provided whenever the function is called. So, instead of using just the URL with its parameters, we must also add a token; for example:

```
https://testkeysfaas.azurewebsites.net/api/HttpTrigger1?code=o/
    dFoKcpqw3aNMuV3uRFi2qLJdVvr226HXlWs8FkFMGwL63J1ie2dw==
```

There are two main levels for keys:

Host
> Defined for the whole Function App

Function
> Defined just for a function

The authLevel parameter can have several values:

anonymous
> Anyone can call the endpoint with no restriction.

function
> A *function-specific key* is required.

admin
> The *master key* is required to call the function.

Figure 7-1 illustrates how you can manage the access key in the Azure Portal when building your app. When you start your app, make sure that you can see all of your deployed functions. Then, in the panel on the left, under the name of the function that you want to edit (in this figure, "HttpTrigger"), click Manage. A new section is displayed, as shown in the figure, and you can add new function keys and host keys, as well as see those that have already been defined.

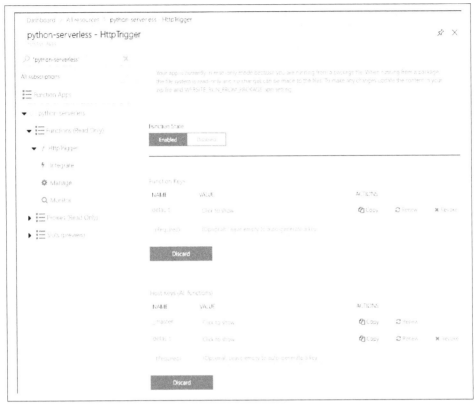

Figure 7-1. Managing access keys in Azure Portal

API Management

If you want additional security added to your endpoints, you can use *API Manager* to add new API endpoints that sit in front of your Function App endpoints. This allows you to do many things, including:

- Mock up calls to your functions when they are still not coded.
- Manage different API versions that call different codebases.
- Group several Function Apps in one API definition.
- Monitor access and set up security and restrictions.

To add an API management layer to your Function App, create a new resource in the Azure Portal of type "API management." Wait for it to be created and then visit the new resource. In the pane on the left side of the screen (see Figure 7-2), select API, and then click Add API. You are then asked for the source of the new API to add; select Function App.

Figure 7-2. Adding an API management layer to a Function App

If you look at the uploaded Function App, you will see a list of all the functions it implements with all of its HTTP methods to import, like the one shown in Figure 7-3.

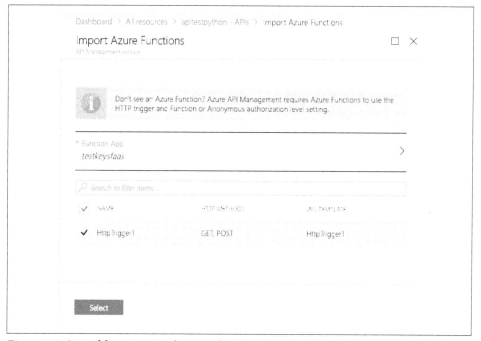

Figure 7-3. List of functions implemented with a Function App, with HTTP methods to import

Select all of them. You'll then be asked for a new display name as well as an API URL suffix for the new API (see Figure 7-4). Also, you are asked whether you want to specify a Product—a collection of several APIs and services to be bundled and versioned together.

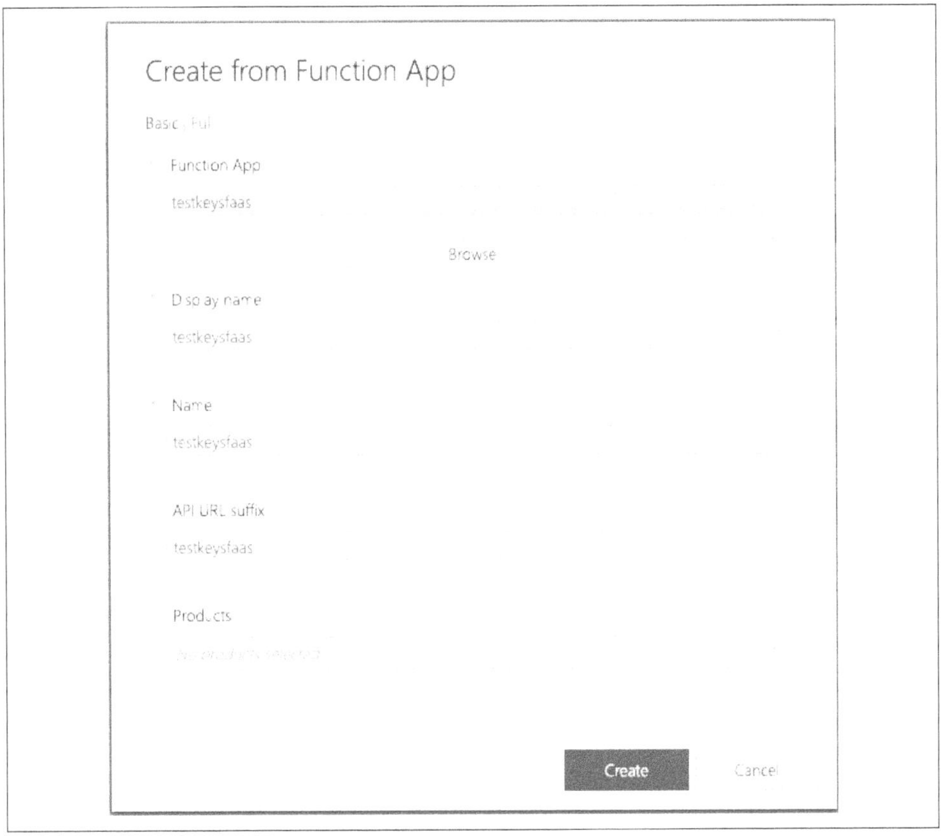

Figure 7-4. *The steps to create new API*

With these steps, you have created a new API management definition. You now can use the many features that this kind of resource implements. Specific to access control and security, you will find the following:

Access control (IAM)
> Add role assignment access to your API.

Users and groups
> Manage a simple list of users if you don't want to rely on more complicated tools for that.

Subscriptions
> Create subscription keys with a scope and active or inactive state to distribute to your users.

Identities
> Specify identity providers to be used to access the API, such as the following:
> - Azure Active Directory
> - Azure Active Directory B2C
> - Facebook
> - Google
> - Microsoft
> - Twitter
> - Username and password

OAuth 2.0
> Add an OAuth2 service to authorize clients.

OpenID Connect
> Add an OpenID provider to be used to authorize clients.

Certification Authority (CA) certificates
> Add new certificates for CAs, as a trusted root or an intermediate party.

Client certificates
> Add certificates that clients can use to authorize their requests.

Delegation
> Use your existing website for signin- and signout-like operations.

Managed service identity
> Register with Azure Active Directory to manage identities.

Virtual network
> Create a virtual network that is used for interaction between several Azure Portal services, so access inside the network is unrestricted, for example.

Protocol settings
> Set several options for cipher and client and backend HTTP and Transport Layer Security (TLS) security.

There are many other useful features in API Manager related to other topics, and we suggest that you check them out.

Azure Security

Azure Security is a specialized service on the Azure platform that provides tools and capabilities to secure your application. Azure Security is an integral tool that manages security for the entire organization, not only for a Function App or API. It provides confidentiality, integrity, and availability of customer data while also enabling transparent accountability.

Azure Security offers a wide array of configurable security options, as illustrated in Figure 7-5, so that you can customize your security to comply with the requirements of your organization. It has a list of built-in features that are organized in six functional areas: operations, applications, storage, networking, compute, and identity.

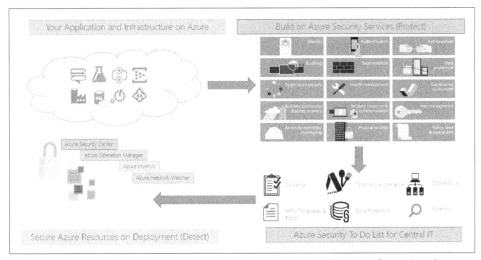

Figure 7-5. An overview of Azure Security (figure courtesy of Microsoft, used with permission)

Operations

The Security and Audit Dashboard provides a quick and clear view of your organizational security. It is a home screen for security related to Log Analytics and provides information about the security of the computers. The following are the components that you can monitor in the Security and Audit Dashboard:

Azure Resource Manager
    Works with resources as a group; with this tool you can deploy, update, or delete all the resources as one operation. This provides security and auditing to your resources. You also can create base templates for the deployments, increasing the security level.

Application Insights

Enables you to monitor your applications and identify possible failures as well as changes in the configuration.

Azure Monitor

Provides visualization, querying, routing, alerting, autoscaling, and automation capabilities. You can configure this tool to alert you in case of security-related events generated in logs.

Log Analytics

Allows you to review metrics and logs, which can be useful in forensics and security analysis. The tool allows you to sift through a large amount of security entries via a query system.

Azure Advisor

A personalized cloud consultant that helps you to optimize your Azure deployments. It analyzes your resource configuration and usage telemetry and provides security recommendations.

Azure Security Center

A unified infrastructure security management system that strengthens the security of your datacenters and provides advanced threat protection across your hybrid workloads in the cloud.

Applications

With Web Application vulnerability scanning, you can test your application's vulnerability with external tools like Tinfoil Security and learn how to improve security and generate reports. Azure has an excellent toolbox for these functions. Here are the main features:

Penetration Testing

Allows you to follow the Azure penetration testing approval process and obtain prior approval to perform the tests.

Web Application firewall (WAF)

Helps to protect applications from common web-based attacks like SQL injection, cross-site scripting (XSS), and session hijacking.

Authentication and authorization in Azure App Service

Provides a way for your application to sign in users so that you don't need to change code on the app backend.

Layered Security Architecture

Provides different levels of network access for each application. Usually the objective is to hide API backends from general internet access.

Web server diagnostics
> Lets you activate different types of logs, like detailed error logging, failed request tracing, and web server logging.

Application diagnostics
> Allows you to capture information produced by a web application. It has two major events: one for application performance, and the other for application failures.

Storage

Role-Based Access Control (RBAC) is a way of managing access to Azure resources. You grant rights by assigning appropriate roles to groups and applications at a certain scope. You can find in this service several tools and features, such as the following:

Shared access signature
> Provides delegated access to resources in the application. This implies that you can grant limited permissions to clients for a specified object over a specified period of time.

Encryption in transit
> A security method that protects data when it is transmitted across the networks. In Azure you can secure data by using transport-level encryption, wire encryption, or client-side encryption.

Data encryption at rest
> In Azure, there are three features that provide this encryption: storage service encryption, client-side encryption, and Azure disk encryption.

Storage analytics
> Performs logging and provides metrics data for a storage account. You can use this data to trace requests, analyze usage trends, and diagnose issues with your storage account.

Cross-origin resource sharing (CORS)
> This is a mechanism that allows domains to give one another permission to access their resources. Azure services support CORS.

Network Layer Controls

Network layer controls limit the connectivity to and from specific devices or subnets. The objective of network access control is to ensure that your virtual machines and services are accessible only to the clients that you want. This service offers several tools and features, including the following:

Network security groups (NSGs)
Basic filtering firewalls for use in controlling traffic moving between subnets

Route control and forced tunneling
Provide major network security and access-control capabilities

Forced tunneling
Ensures that your services are not allowed to initiate a connection to devices on the internet

User-defined routes
Allow you to customize inbound and outbound paths for traffic moving into and out of VMs or subnets to guarantee the most secure route possible

The previous configurations and security techniques provide security at the network and transport layer of the OSI model.

Azure Virtual Network is a representation of your own network in the cloud. Using this representation you can control several aspects of your network, such as IP address blocks, DNS settings, security policies, and route tables.

VPN Gateway is a type of virtual network that sends encrypted traffic across a public connection.

Networking

For general networking services, the following services are available:

- Azure ExpressRoute is a dedicated WAN link that lets you extend your network into the Microsoft cloud over a dedicated private connection. These types of connections do not go over the public internet, so they can be considered more secure than VPN-based solutions.

- Azure Application Gateway provides an application delivery controller (ADC) as a service offering load-balancing and routing capabilities includingHTTP load balancing, cookie-based sessions, and Secure Sockets Layer (SSL) encryption.

- WAF is a feature of Azure Application Gateway. This provides protection to a web application against most of the Open Web Application Security Project (OWASP) Top 10 vulnerabilities.

- Azure Traffic Manager allows you to control the distribution of the client's traffic between several datacenters. Traffic Manager uses DNS to redirect client requests to better endpoints based on traffic routing and the health of the endpoints.

- Azure Load Balancer is a layer 4 load balancer (Transmission Control Protocol [TCP]/User Datagram Protocol [UDP]) that distributes incoming traffic between healthy instances. It has several configurations:

  — Load-balance incoming internet traffic to VMs.

  — Load-balance traffic between VMs in a virtual network.

  — Forward external traffic to a specific VM.

- Internal DNS and Azure DNS give you the ability to resolve a website or a service name to its IP address.

- Azure Security Center provides unified security management and advanced threat protection across hybrid cloud workloads. It helps to prevent, detect, and respond to threats and provides increased visibility into and control over the security of your Azure resources.

## CHAPTER 8

Monitoring

Whenever you deploy a cloud-based application that processes many different user requests or runs a long batch calculation, monitoring its evolution is essential.

You need to keep a log of all of the different actions that involve your system as well as each request so that you can review and analyze them. You might detect that something is taking longer than it should and that one of the steps is bottlenecking the entire system. You might also want to get automatic alerts when something is not working properly so that a responsible technician can act on it.

In this final chapter, we focus on how you can use Azure Monitor to ensure that you have insight into how your serverless project is performing.

Azure Monitor

Because we are using the Azure cloud infrastructure for our serverless solutions, we can rely on the Azure Monitor service.

Azure Monitor is a solution for collecting telemetry data and analyzing it in a cloud environment. With Azure Monitor, you can understand how your cloud applications are performing and identify possible issues affecting them.

An Azure Monitor configuration for a project can be divided into three different aspects, as depicted in Figure 8-1: the storage of all the data for metrics and logs, the analysis and alerting functionality, and log streaming to other systems.

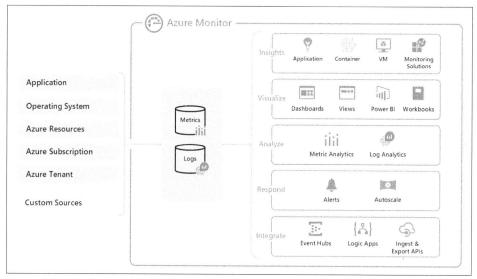

Figure 8-1. Overview of Azure Monitor (figure courtesy of Microsoft, used with permission)

To access Azure Monitor, go to the Azure Portal and select Monitor in the pane on the left side of the window, or look for it in the "All services" section. You can then start inspecting metrics and logs as well as set up new sources of data. Figure 8-2 shows all of the elements that you can find in Azure Monitor.

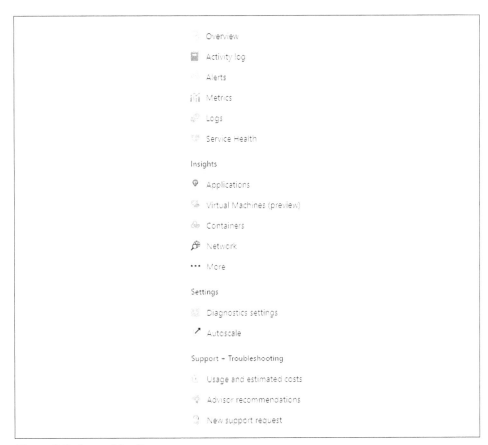

Figure 8-2. Azure Monitor

Metrics and Logs

Azure Monitor defines two types of data: *metrics* and *logs*. All of the data processed belongs to one of these categories.

Metrics are numerical values that describe an aspect of a system at a particular point in time. This data is usually lightweight and used in near-real-time scenarios. Azure Monitor has a component called Azure Monitor Metrics Explorer with which you can observe this kind of data during maintenance of the project.

Logs are different types of data, organized in records with different sets of properties. These records are stored in Log Analytics, which uses its own query language to consolidate and analyze stored data.

Data Sources

Azure Monitor can obtain and store data from different sources: your own cloud application, the Azure services it relies on, or even other external cloud services. All of the sources are organized in tiers, and each one can have multiple types of data as well as services to ingest and analyze that data.

The tiers, with their respective services and features, are as follows:

Azure tenant
> Telemetry for the Microsoft identity platform and Azure Active Directory.

> *Azure Active Directory Audit Logs*
>> History of sign-in activity and audit trail of changes made within a particular tenant.

Azure platform/subscription
> Health and operation of Azure itself. With this, you can monitor how the Azure platform is performing without taking into consideration your own apps. If the platform is slow or down, the problem is not that your app is not optimized. Rather, the problem is with the platform itself. This rarely happens, but with this data you can be sure everything is working properly in Azure.

> *Azure Service Health*
>> Health of the Azure services in your subscription on which your application and resources rely.

> *Azure Activity Log*
>> Service health records along with records on any configuration changes made to your Azure resources. If someone authorized makes changes to the configuration of your services, you can review a log of these activities.

Azure resources
> Metrics and resource-level diagnostic logs providing information about the internal operation of Azure resources.

> *Metrics*
>> Platform metrics that reflect the performance and operation of Azure services.

> *Resource Diagnostic Logs*
>> Logs providing insights into the operation of the resource itself.

> *Monitoring Solutions*
>> Data to provide additional insight into the operation of a particular service or application.

Guest OS
> A compute resource that relies on a guest operating system, in Azure or another cloud provider, that can be monitored with the installation of agents to gather telemetry.

> *Azure Diagnostics extension*
>> Basic level of monitoring for client operating system of Azure compute resources.

> *Log Analytics agent*
>> Comprehensive monitoring and management of your Windows or Linux VMs or physical computer.

> *Dependency agent*
>> Service Map and Azure Monitor for VMs require a Dependency agent on Windows and Linux VMs. It integrates with the Log Analytics agent to collect discovered data about processes running on the virtual machine and external process dependencies.

Applications
> Data from your applications, regardless of the platform they're running on. This data is collected using Application Insights.

> *Application data*
>> By installing an instrumentation package, you can collect log data sent directly from within your application.

> *Dependencies*
>> If you need to collect telemetry from across multiple components, Application Insights supports distributed telemetry correlation; this identifies the dependencies between components, allowing you to analyze them together.

> *Availability tests*
>> You can test the availability and responsiveness of your application from different locations on the public internet.

Custom sources
> Any data that must be collected that is not covered in the other tiers.

> *Data Collector API*
>> You can collect log data from any REST client to extend monitoring to resources that don't expose telemetry through other sources.

Application Insights

Application Insights helps you to understand how your app is performing and how it is being used. It is an Application Performance Management (APM) tool, and to use it, you need to install an instrumentation package in your application. This package monitors your application and sends telemetry to the portal. The impact to the application is minimal.

Figure 8-3 shows an example in which a web application with several components, using the instrumentation package, sends telemetry to the Application Insights service. You can then use this data in different ways: send alerts, explore the data using Power BI, access it within the Visual Studio IDE, consume it via the RESTful API interface, or set up a continuous export to some other storage, like a CSV file or a database.

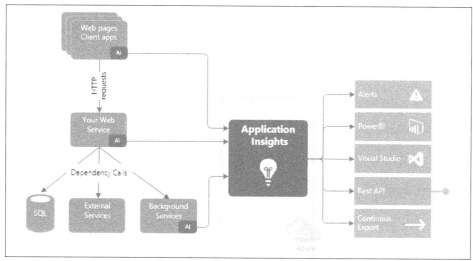

Figure 8-3. Overview of Application Insights (figure courtesy of Microsoft, used with permission)

Insights for Containers (and VMs)

Azure Monitor for containers is a feature designed to monitor the performance of container workloads deployed to either Azure Container Instances or managed Kubernetes clusters hosted on Azure Kubernetes Service.

You can use it to collect container logs as well as memory and processor metrics from controllers, nodes, and containers that are available in Kubernetes through the Metrics API. This will be useful to you when you want to monitor your Kubernetes cluster with your custom machine learning containers so that you can do the following:

- Monitor containers that are running on the node and their average processor and memory utilization, and identify resource bottlenecks.

- Monitor processor and memory utilization of container groups and their containers.

- Identify where the container resides in a controller or a Pod and review the controller's or Pod's overall performance.

- Review the resource utilization of workloads running on the host that are unrelated to the standard processes that support the Pod.

- Understand the behavior of the cluster under different loads and identify the maximum load the cluster can sustain.

You can access Azure Monitor for containers' data from the main Azure Monitor page, or on the Azure Kubernetes page when selecting an AKS cluster, or for a selected AKS container. A similar service for VMs exists: Azure Monitor for VMs.

Log Analytics

Log data collected in Azure Monitor is stored in a Log Analytics workspace. This store has telemetry from different sources, and you can use the Data Explorer Query Language to retrieve, filter, combine, and analyze the data.

The data is stored in different partitions and dedicated tables in the Log Analytics workspace. To access this data, you must use the Application Insights console or the Application Insights REST API.

Data Explorer Query Language

Azure Monitor uses Data Explorer Query Language to search for and retrieve data from the Log Analytics workspace. You can use it for simple queries that you write for quick insights as well as for complex queries that must take into consideration many different system parameters.

Here's what a Data Explorer query looks like:

```
requests
| where timestamp > ago(24h) and success=="False"
| join kind=inner (exceptions
        | where timestamp > ago(24h) ) on operation_Id
| project type, method, requestName = name, requestDuration = duration
```

As you can see, it uses entities that are similar to SQL, organized in a hierarchy using a tabular expression. Here, we are selecting stored data from "requests" that have been monitored, whose timestamp value is greater than 24 hours ago and that didn't succeed. We mix this query with data from "exceptions" that have also been logged for the same `operation_Id` identifier more than 24 hours ago. We also indicate in the query that we want to know the project type, the method, the `requestName` (renamed to `name`), and the `requestDuration` (renamed to `duration`).

Alerts

In Azure Monitor, you can set up notifications for critical conditions and actions to attempt to correct them before your system's users notice.

Alert rules in Azure Monitor use *action groups*, as shown in Figure 8-4, which contain unique sets of recipients and actions that can be shared across multiple rules. Based on your requirements, action groups can perform such actions as using webhooks to kick-start external actions or to integrate with your own IT service management tools.

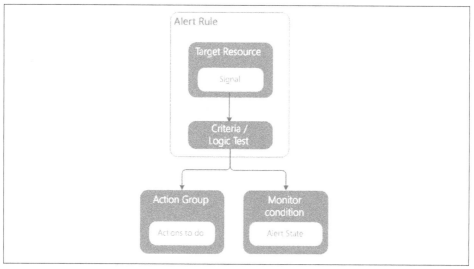

Figure 8-4. Overview of Azure Monitor Alerts (figure courtesy of Microsoft, used with permission)

Smart Groups

One of the biggest challenges with alerts is to identify real problems in the data received. *Smart groups* are automatically created by using machine learning algorithms to combine related alerts that represent a single issue. When an alert is created, the algorithm adds it to a new smart group or an existing smart group based on information such as historical patterns, similar properties, and similar structure. The smart group detail page provides information about the group, including the reasoning used to create the group.

Autoscale and Metrics Alerts

Autoscale is what allows you to have the appropriate amount of resources running to handle the load of the application. You can define a minimum and maximum number of instances, and you can scale automatically between those two values using rules that you create.

Metrics alerts evaluate, at regular intervals, whether one or more conditions of one or more metrics are true, and then send notifications when the conditions are met. You can define a metric alert rule by specifying a target resource to be monitored, the metric name, and the condition and an action group to be triggered when the alert rule fires.

Index

example architecture, 13
external storage, 100
Jupyter Notebook in, 108
Kubernetes Secrets, 101
machine learning tools for, 102-104
resources, 99
scaling, 101
single container machine learning, 105

L

layered security architecture, 118
load-balancing, 120
local development environment, 48-52
  Azure Functions Core Tools, 49
  .NET Core v2.x, 48
  Node.js, 49
  package manager, 49
  Python 3.6, 50-52
local.settings.json file, 57
Log Analytics, 127, 129-131
Logic Apps, 36
logistic regression, 76
logs, 125

M

machine learning and deep learning models
  advances in artificial intelligence, 3
  Azure Cognitive Services, 71-75
  benefits of containers for, 12
  benefits of serverless computing for, 13
  challenges of, 4, 8
  cloud machine learning solutions, 81-89
  deep learning basics, 7
  definition of machine learning, vii, 3
  distributed machine learning, 108
  general machine learning tools, 75-80
  Kubernetes machine learning tools, 102-104
  machine learning basics, 3-7
  neural networks in, 7
  serverless machine learning basics, 10
  single container machine learning, 105
Machine Learning Studio
  application options, 82
  benefits of, 36
  data science activities, 81
  predictive example, 83-86
  training model data workflow, 84
Mercurial, 94
metrics and logs, 125, 126

microservices architecture, 18, 23
Microsoft Azure (see Azure)
Microsoft Azure Application Gateway, 120
Microsoft Azure ExpressRoute, 120
Microsoft Cognitive Toolkit, 75
ML.NET, 77
Modified National Institute of Standards and
  Technology (MNIST) dataset, 80
monitoring
  Application Insights, 128
  Azure Monitor, 123
  data source, 126
  Log Analytics, 129-131
  metrics and logs, 125
monolithic architecture, 18
multi-layer artificial neural networks, 7

N

.NET Core v2.x, 48
network layer controls, 119
network security groups (NSGs), 120
Networking services, 120
neural networks, 7
Node Version Manager tool (nvm), 49
Node.js, 20, 49

O

object-oriented programming (OOP), 20, 21
OneDrive, 94
Open Neural Network Exchange Format
  (ONNX), 81
overfitting, 10

P

package managers, 49
penetration testing, 118
perceptrons, 7
pip tool, 52
pipeline structures, 103
Pix2Story, 6
Pods, 99
predictive analytics, 81
price prediction, 77
process.env variable, 58
product recommendation, 77
production settings, 57
pure functions, 20
pyenv tool, 52

About the Authors

Vicente Herrera García is a seasoned software engineer with solid experience in all facets of software and web development. He possesses a master's degree in computer science from the University of Seville and is highly skilled in collaborating with clients to achieve technical, business, and financial objectives. Vicente is adept at streamlining processes, enhancing productivity levels, and introducing new emerging methodologies that enrich product development. A certified Expert Level Scrum Master, he is a certification teacher and examiner at Scrum Manager, and he also teaches software, web development, and project management at the University of Seville and other private institutions.

John Biggs is an entrepreneur, consultant, writer, and maker. He spent 15 years as an editor for Gizmodo, CrunchGear, and TechCrunch and has a deep background in hardware startups, 3D printing, and the blockchain. His work has appeared in *Men's Health*, *Wired*, and the *New York Times*. He runs the *Technotopia* podcast about a better future. John has written five books, including the best book on blogging, *Bloggers Boot Camp* (Focal Press), and a book about the most expensive timepiece ever made, *Marie Antoinette's Watch* (CreateSpace). He lives in Brooklyn, New York.

Colophon

The animal on the cover of *Building Intelligent Cloud Applications* is an azure jay (*Cyanocorax caeruleus*). This bird is a member of the crow family, found in the forests of southeastern Brazil, Paraguay, and Argentina. It has a distinctive blue body with a black head and neck. The jay is about 16 inches long and weighs around 9.5 ounces.

Azure jays are omnivorous, with a diet of insects, seeds, and fruit. They especially favor the nut-like seeds of the Paraná pine (*Araucaria angustifolia*) and play a role in seed dispersal in the tree's lifecycle—they carry the seeds elsewhere to eat, and bury cones that later sprout. As with other corvid species, these birds are very intelligent and social. They live in small multigenerational groups, and have a variety of distinct calls to communicate information.

The azure jay is the official bird of the Brazilian state of Paraná. In the same region, there is a folktale about the Gralha Azul (Blue Crow), where a black crow is saddened by the destruction of the forests and makes a pact with an angel to plant new trees, in exchange for gaining brilliant blue plumage. Based on the behavior of actual azure jays, this character is a symbol of environmental stewardship.

Many of the animals on O'Reilly covers are endangered; all of them are important to the world.

The cover illustration is by Karen Montgomery, based on an image from Temminck and Laugier's *New Collection of Colored Plates of Birds*. The cover fonts are Gilroy Semibold and Guardian Sans. The text font is Adobe Minion Pro; the heading font is Adobe Myriad Condensed; and the code font is Dalton Maag's Ubuntu Mono.

O'REILLY®

There's much more where this came from.

Experience books, videos, live online training courses, and more from O'Reilly and our 200+ partners—all in one place.

Learn more at oreilly.com/online-learning

Lightning Source UK Ltd.
Milton Keynes UK
UKHW030121130919

349659UK00005B/8/P